PLURALISM AND PEACE

In *Pluralism and Peace,* John May brings a wide and deep knowledge of Asian, Melanesian and Australian indigenous religion to bear on key questions concerning civil society and democratic government in our world. Highly conversant with both German and English-speaking debates, May shows how the cause of a global civil society needs to draw inspiration and sustenance from religious traditions, avoiding the impoverishments of secularist ideology, while religions themselves must challenge their own fundamentalisms and propensity to generate violence. *Pluralism and Peace* is an impressive and convincing argument on behalf of peaceful engagement between the faiths and moral commitments that guide our lives.

Dr Robert Gascoigne
Emeritus Professor
School of Theology
Australian Catholic University

In this very timely and important book, *Pluralism and Peace: The Religions in Global Civil Society*, John D'Arcy May explores how the resurgent religions throughout Asia and the Pacific can work together to undercut outbreaks of violence and terrorism claiming a religious sanction. Drawing from his extensive scholarship, May writes that religions must divest themselves of past sectarianism and fundamentalist extremism and develop a global theology, building foundations for peace without destroying their identities and cultures. He sees the way forward with the religions inspiring practical collaboration in areas such as conflict resolution, economic development, health care and education. He warns that "the task is urgent: it concerns nothing less than humankind's continued existence on this threatened planet".

Dr Bruce Duncan CSsR,
Yarra Theological Union
University of Divinity.

With extremist movements of all persuasions threatening peace in today's fragile world, this book, wide-ranging in scope, will appeal to the thinking person. Does religion have any role to play in promoting peace in our global civic society today? The author is well equipped with his rich knowledge and international experience in Ireland, Europe, Asia, and Australia, to explore these and related questions. His summary of the history of democracy in selected Asian countries and how they have dealt with religion is particularly interesting. Looking to the future the author suggests some ways of how interactive theology, done collaboratively in a multifaith context, might provide a new theology to meet the urgent contemporary quest for ethically responsible globalisation.

Dr Gideon Goosen
Theologian, ecumenist and author
Emeritus Professor
Australian Catholic University.

PLURALISM & PEACE

THE RELIGIONS IN GLOBAL CIVIL SOCIETY

JOHN D'ARCY MAY

COVENTRY
PRESS

Published in Australia by
Coventry Press
33 Scoresby Road
Bayswater Vic. 3153
Australia

ISBN 9780648497783

Copyright © John D'Arcy May 2019

All rights reserved. Other than for the purposes and subject to the conditions prescribed under the *Copyright Act*, no part of this publication may be reproduced, stored in a retrieval system, or transmitted in any form or by any means, electronic, mechanical, photocopying, recording or otherwise, without the prior permission of the publisher.

Cataloguing-in-Publication entry is available from the National Library of Australia http:/catalogue.nla.gov.au/.

Design by Film Shot Graphics
Cover design by Ian James – www.jgd.com.au

Printed in Australia

Dedicated to the memory of

Rev. Michael Hurley SJ

and

Rev. Robin H. S. Boyd

Pioneers of the ecumenical in all its dimensions

Contents

Foreword xiii
Introduction: An Asia-Pacific Perspective 1

PART I
THE ORIGINS OF CIVIL SOCIETY

Chapter 1: The Religious Roots of Democracy 15

1.1 Origins and Transformations of Civil Society 16
1.2 Democracy and Civil Society 19
1.3 From Religious to Political Pluralism. 25

Chapter 2: Globalisation and Westernisation 31

2.1 'Why do they hate us so much?' 32
2.2 Civil Society in Non-Western Contexts. 38
2.3 Globalisation of Religion? 42

PART II
THE RELIGIONS IN ASIA-PACIFIC SOCIETIES

Chapter 3: Religious Plurality and Democracy 49
          (Indonesia and Thailand)

3.1 Democracy and Diversity in Indonesia 50
3.2 Buddhism and Democracy in Thailand. 59
3.3 The Deeper Dimensions of Democratic Pluralism. 65

Chapter 4: Buddhism, Peace and Violence 73
          (Sri Lanka and Japan)

4.1 The Radicalisation of Buddhism in Sri Lanka 74
4.2 Buddhism and Japanese Imperialism. 81
4.3 Pacifism and the Religions 87

Chapter 5: Land and Life as Religious Values 93
    (Australia and Melanesia)

5.1 Land as the Presence of Spirit: The Aborigines 94
5.2 Wellbeing and Community: The Melanesians 102
5.3 Land as the Basis of Interreligious Communication 106

Chapter 6: Economic Ethics: Globalising Values? 111
    (Melanesia and Thailand)

6.1 Reciprocity and Retribution in Melanesia 114
6.2 Spirit and Money in Buddhism 121
6.3 Globalisation and the Plurality of Values 126

Chapter 7: Refugees: Humans Without Rights? 131
    (Indonesia and Australia)

7.1 Transit and *Transmigrasi* in Indonesia 133
7.2 Australia: The Great Refusal 138
7.3 Compassion and Action 147

Part III
The Globalisation of Theology: Relativising the Religions?

Chapter 8: Collaborative Theologies? 151

8.1 Comparative Theology 152
8.2 Collaborative Theology 160
8.3 Global Theology? 164

Chapter 9: The Ecumenical Imperative 171

9.1 Democracy as the Institutionalisation of Justice 177
9.2 Ecumenical Religion and Economics 182
9.3 Global Reflexivity 186

Bibliography 189

Da es nun mit der unter den Völkern der Erde einmal durchgängig überhandgenommenen (engeren oder weiteren) Gemeinschaft so weit gekommen ist, daß die Rechtsverletzung an *einem* Platz der Erde an *allen* gefühlt wird; so ist die Idee eines Weltbürgerrechts keine phantastische und überspannte Vorstellungsart des Rechts, sondern eine notwendige Ergänzung des ungeschriebenen Kodex, sowohl des Staats- als Völkerrechts zum öffentlichen Menschenrechte überhaupt, und so zum ewigen Frieden, zu dem man sich in der kontinuierlichen Annäherung zu befinden, nur unter dieser Bedingung schmeicheln darf.

> Immanuel Kant, *Zum ewigen Frieden. Ein philosophischer Entwurf* (1795), *Dritter Definitivartikel.*

The peoples of the earth have now gone a good distance in forming themselves into smaller or larger communities; this has gone so far that a violation of rights in one place is now felt throughout the world. So the idea of a law of world citizenship is not a legal flight of fancy; rather, it is necessary to complete the unwritten code of civil and international law and also mankind's written laws; and so it is needed for perpetual peace. Until we can establish a law of world citizenship, we mustn't congratulate ourselves on how close we are coming to that.

> Immanuel Kant, *Towards Perpetual Peace: A Philosophical Sketch* (1795), Third Definitive Article.

Foreword

In the Winter Semester of 2015, I had the privilege and pleasure of being invited for the second time to be the visiting professor in the Johann Wolfgang Goethe University of Frankfurt's innovative program *Theologie interkulturell*. For over thirty years my friends and colleagues in the Faculty of Catholic Theology have invited a theologian from a country outside Western Europe to give a series of lectures and seminars on theology in his or her cultural context. The published lectures have created a veritable library of indigenous and contextual theologies.

My host, the current program chair, Professor Thomas Schreijäck, and his staff did everything possible to make my stay in Frankfurt fruitful and enjoyable. I wish to thank them and also the students who engaged in lively discussions in my seminars, especially on the day after the Paris attacks of 13 November 2015. The 'founding fathers' of the program attended the lectures and interrogated me about them at supper in the *Mensa* afterwards.

The lectures were published as *Die Religionen in der globalen Zivilgesellschaft. Eine Asien-Pazifik-Perspektive* (Ostfildern: Matthias Grünewald Verlag, 2017). The present volume is a considerably augmented and updated translation, which I hope Australian readers in particular will find relevant and interesting. 2015, the year of the so-called 'refugee crisis' and Germany's spontaneous and generous response to it, was an historic moment to be in Europe. This book tries to address some of the questions it raised for both politics and theology.

I particularly wish to thank Dr Bruce Duncan of Yarra Theological Union, University of Divinity, Melbourne, for invaluable advice on issues that developed before I returned to Australia; Dr Anita Ray of Australian Catholic University, Melbourne, for confirming that I have indeed reaped the fruits of the working group on comparative theology which she convened; and Professor Robert Gascoigne of Australian Catholic University, Sydney, for helpful comments on my attempt to portray faiths in the public sphere. Any remaining shortcomings and mistakes are entirely my own. Finally, Hugh McGinlay has once again been a sympathetic and encouraging publisher.

Introduction: An Asia-Pacific Perspective

At an ecumenical conference, the participants were broken up into regional groupings, one of which was 'Asia-Pacific'. The first thing the members of this group asked was, "Why are we together?" The term Asia-Pacific does seem remarkably abstract, like an artificial attempt to bring the enormous cultural and religious variety of the region under a common denominator. Is this another example of a Western category being imposed on very diverse cultures with their own inherited ways of conducting politics? This is a question to which we shall return.

In the foreground, however, will be the religions themselves. All the world's major religions, broadly speaking, have their origins in Asia, and around the vast expanse of the Pacific Ocean may be found examples of just about every type of indigenous religion. Not only that: they are all interacting in increasingly complicated ways. Modern media of communication, opportunities for travel and trade relationships are binding this bewildering variety of languages, ethnicities and religious cultures together, despite the inevitable tensions and clashes when cultures intermingle. But the dynamic thus set in train may have unpredictable outcomes. Inasmuch as civil society exists in these national contexts – albeit in contrasting forms – some political scientists maintain that a wider civil society is taking shape which has global implications. Our question will be: are relationships among the religions being changed in this new context, either positively, in that their growing awareness of one another makes them more open, or negatively, by making them retreat into intensified fundamentalisms? Is interreligious communication in global civil society changing the nature of religious and theological pluralism?

It is scarcely possible to do theology in Australia without taking into account the Asia-Pacific – and more recently, the Indo-Pacific – contexts. The two rapidly developing superpowers of the region, China and India ('Chindia'), dominate this context, but each of these enormous and enormously complex countries demands far more attention than can be given them in this study. Like the Himalayas, however – the huge mountain range that separates them – they will always be visible on the horizon. We are not so much interested in geopolitics as in the ways the religions and their theologies are beginning to relate to one another in this rapidly changing context. Nevertheless, we need to remind ourselves that, with the exception of Christianity, which arrived in the region relatively late, and Islam, with its origins in Arabia, the most influential religious traditions of Northeast and Southeast Asia – Hinduism, Buddhism, Daoism and Confucianism – derive their practices and beliefs from Indian and Chinese culture. In this sense, their influence in the Asia-Pacific may be compared to that of Greece and Rome on the cultures of Europe. China and India are becoming economically, politically and militarily – and in subtle ways culturally and spiritually as well – more important. Against this background, we shall be studying the developing interreligious relationships in the Asia-Pacific and their implications for Christian and other theologies.

A religious ecology of the region would reveal that in many conflict situations the religions have been prepared to engage in dialogue and reconciliation, but their potential to incite violence is equally undeniable. The rise and fall of Islamic State is perhaps the most dramatic example of this, but Hindus, Buddhists and Christians are also guilty of perpetrating violent acts of persecution and even ethnic cleansing against other faith communities and ethnic groups. In Indonesia and Japan, Myanmar and Sri Lanka,

Introduction

there have been appalling examples of complicity between religious traditions and state-sponsored racist ethnocentrism. When such ethnic-religious nationalism gains the upper hand in Southeast Asia, or tribal loyalties are put before the national interest on the Pacific Islands, democracy itself is compromised, and it is subjected to further pressure by the streams of refugees within the region itself and from the Middle East.

One of the main themes of this study will be the ways in which the relationships of the religions among themselves interact with the emergence of the civil society that makes these relationships possible. Civil society – as the free space for human fulfilment, cultural development and political activity – is the indispensable presupposition of democracy, but in many Asia-Pacific countries it is fragile and threatened. At the same time, nevertheless, we may be seeing a *global* civil society taking shape, which, thanks to modern communications media, can circumvent the repressive measures of authoritarian governments and establish itself as an international forum for the expression of opinion and political involvement. This process is not the same as so-called globalisation, which has to do mainly with economic and financial activities, but it gives reason to hope that globalisation can be ethically responsible.

The religions, far from being the fossilised remains of a distant past, could prove to be the non-renewable *spiritual* resources that make ethical globalisation possible. Before they can play this role, however, they must divest themselves of their historical baggage of mutual antagonism, violent sectarianism, fundamentalist extremism and refusal of genuine pluralism. For this, a new type of collaborative theology will be necessary, a *global* theology, which will open up ways of peaceful cooperation without destroying the distinctive identities of religions and cultures. This is without doubt a difficult task, which the present book can only hint at.

But the task is urgent: it concerns nothing less than humankind's continued existence on this threatened planet. What, then, could be the starting points of a strategy for the religions in the new situation created by global civil society?

The two most bitterly debated documents of the Second Vatican Council (1962-1965) were the Declaration on the Relationship of the Church to Non-Christian Religions, *Nostra Aetate* (28 October 1965) and the Declaration on Religious Freedom, *Dignitatis Humanae* (7 December 1965). As the date of its promulgation indicates, *Dignitatis Humanae* was one of the very last documents to be approved by the Council, after many controversies and revisions. It was contested because it seemed to introduce an 'American' view of democratic pluralism and human rights into a church whose historical ideal of its rightful position was the intimate relationship between church and state in a country like Spain, reflected in a number of Latin American dictatorships and summed up in the infamous slogan 'Error has no rights'.

But *Nostra Aetate* was also resisted and its genesis was even more complex. Its innovation was to reflect on the church's relationship with the Jews in the context, not of Christian ecumenism (which was eventually treated in a separate document, the Decree on Ecumenism, *Unitatis Redintegratio*), but of all the world's religions. There were no precedents for this. In view of the Arab-Israeli conflict, the whole matter was politically charged, and though the document scrupulously avoids even mentioning the State of Israel, its very existence heralded a new era in the awareness of Judaism in Christian theology and in the Vatican's relations with the Jewish State.

The two documents are entitled 'declarations' because they are explicitly addressed *ad extra*, to the international community of states and religions outside the purview of the Roman Catholic Church. Read together, they amount to a linking of international relations and interreligious relations, indeed – though it could hardly have been expressed this way in a document of the Magisterium – to a charter for pluralism, both political and religious. The potential implicit in the synergy of *Nostra Aetate* and *Dignitatis Humanae* has come nowhere near being realised in the more than fifty years since the Council.

The transformation of civil society, one of the fundamental presuppositions of democracy, into a *global* communicative milieu has also transformed the conditions under which the religions become aware of one another and relate to one another. It has also gone hand in hand with a weakening of democracy in those countries in which it seemed most securely established.

In the Asia-Pacific, these transformations are becoming evident in the ways in which very different states with very different religious cultures are developing and interacting. Observing this process, we realise that religions are unavoidably public and political, even and perhaps especially when they try to abstain from politics.

According to Hegel, civil society is that dimension of the public arena which mediates between the private sphere of the family and the official institutions of the state. The concept is characteristic of modernity and has its roots in the European Enlightenment. It designates an open space for the free expression of opinion, the creation of organisations, political activity and not least personal development and creativity. It is precisely this scope for the exercise of freedom that makes civil society so threatening to totalitarian and authoritarian regimes. Civil society, as the self-regulating interaction of citizens, can only be restricted and controlled by the use of force, as we have seen in China and

Russia. Its hallmark is civility, at once the greatest achievement and the presupposition of democratic societies.

But democracy, not least in the countries of its most impressive development in the Old World and the New, is in the grip of a deepening crisis. Many people in the West are becoming weary of democracy because the established political parties seem ever more similar and are perceived to be influenced by aggressive advertising, economic interests and electoral manipulation, leading to the creation and rapid growth of more extreme alternatives.

In Africa, despite the triumph of democracy over apartheid in South Africa, the states set up by colonial powers are constantly subverted by corrupt politicians and generals, hungry for power. The Arab Spring has ended disastrously in most Muslim countries. How then has civil society fared in the democracies of the Asia-Pacific – for all the countries we shall be discussing are democratic in one way or another – and what role do the religions play in them?

The religions of the region face massive challenges, which we shall be discussing in some detail. Economic upheaval, climate change, environmental destruction, threats to peace, the movement of refugees – the list is long. Less familiar, perhaps, is the fact that the religions often present the greatest problem *for one another*. Ideally, they should be a source of hope and motivation for meeting these challenges, but in reality the religions are often more preoccupied with themselves than with the problems of globalisation.

The present study sets itself the daunting task of investigating the indispensability of theology for the encounter of religions. The effectiveness and credibility of the religions have deeper spiritual roots which are not easy to discover, but the means by which they give expression to their faith, their hope and their capacity for love are conceptual, in other words: theological. Great theologies

Introduction

are the result of grappling with great problems. By no means all religions, of course, use the term 'theology', but this difficulty is not insurmountable. It is much more important to construct methodologies by which the theologians of the most disparate traditions could do theology *together*, collaboratively. Here, I shall propose, lies the deeper meaning of the somewhat jaded term 'ecumenical'.

The thesis that a *global* civil society is taking shape remains controversial. As we shall see, some political scientists believe it is a chimera, a sociological fantasy. Others – and I am inclined to agree with them – see in this development an epoch-making change in modes of communication and political activity. Accompanying this is a change, not only in the modalities of interreligious discourse, but in the plausibility of religious language itself. This will be our hypothesis as we contemplate the great religious communities of the Asia-Pacific region, above all Buddhism, Christianity and Islam, but also, and in close interrelationship with these, the numerous 'little' traditions characteristic of indigenous or *primal* religion.

Despite the loud objections of the 'New Atheists' and other secularists, most human beings are religious in one sense or another, and the number of persons who are religious in some sense is steadily increasing, not decreasing. In their religiosity can be discerned one or other form of this 'primal' religion, which celebrates and sustains physical life itself and makes it meaningful. It is the indispensable basis, not only of human existence in such cultures, but of the sustainability of the 'great' traditions, which always and everywhere maintain themselves in an intimate symbiosis with it. Secular discourse too, when it is philosophically self-reflective, opens up transcendent perspectives which are not unrelated to those of religion.

What I envisage, then, is a kind of 'religious ecology' of the Asia-Pacific. Ecological awareness properly so called is fundamental to this, for the destruction of the environment is the source of many other crises and problems. The religions, in fact, are closely interwoven with the life contexts and cultures of the region. Among other things, this means that in the public sphere, whether they like it or not, the utterances and activities of the religions are unavoidably political. This would seem to imply that the global public sphere, unlike its state-based precedents in Western countries, is not necessarily 'neutral' or 'secular'. Rather, it will be found to have an underlying religious component, which is difficult for those with an education biased towards the secular to see. In this context, 'religious' does not connote something static or passive, but a dynamic of constantly changing interactions. The religions of the Asia-Pacific are involved in a process of mutual transformation in the context of profound changes in the region's economic and military equilibrium. At bottom, this amounts to a struggle of ethnic and religious identities. This competition can, of course, result in violent conflict, of which we shall see many examples. But the religions can also inspire one another to take initiatives in areas such as conflict resolution, economic development, health care and education. They can be the guardians of the traditional values of conservatism in the best sense, not necessarily reactionary but innovative and progressive.

The public assertion of truth which is meant to be binding on the members of a society or organisation is at the same time an exercise of power. The claim to truth and the enjoyment of freedom are not easy to reconcile in the institutional structures of society. Truth that is regarded as necessary for the coherence and continuance of organisations, from political parties to empires, becomes ideology by virtue of the powerful interests which appropriate it. Religious institutions such as the Buddhist *sangha*, the councils of the early church or the Islamic caliphate are no exception to this. All three factors – truth, power and ideology – shore up the identity of religious communities and make it seem unassailable.

Interreligious communication, therefore, by no means consists solely in the transmission of truths, as the missionaries of different religions tend to believe. It is always fraught with claims to power, which are bound up with convictions of superiority and can humiliate and alienate those subjected to them. Not only that: the cognitive content of religious discourse is unconsciously determined by pre-conceptual symbols and archetypes, whose potential for turning doctrine into ideology is usually not recognised.

If communication is to succeed, the religions must become aware of the deep symbolic structures from which the metaphors and concepts of their language derive. If the theologies of the various religions are to gain validity in the process of global communication, they will have to explore these dimensions of their self-understanding, not *against* one another, as so often happens, but *with* one another. Only thus, I wish to maintain, can theology become global, globalisation ethical and civil society humane. Our quest is to discover whether and to what extent this is likely to happen in the Asia-Pacific.

We may now preview the shape our study will take. First of all, we must clarify the concept of civil society, its origins in the Enlightenment and its persistence under the changing conditions of globalisation, always with the question in mind whether civil society is necessarily a 'secular' category (Part I). We shall look at the plurality of worldviews as a factor in democratic stability and the implications of religious pluralism for the truth claims of the religions and their theologies (Chapter 1). The globalisation of civil society brings into focus the relationships of different societies in the region to 'the West': does this mean the ineluctable westernisation and secularisation of these cultures? (Chapter 2).

We must then move out into the vastness of the Asia-Pacific, engaging in selective case studies of the metamorphoses of religions in the process of globalisation and the metaphors with which they seek to cope with these changes (Part II). We will examine the strengths and weaknesses of democracy in Indonesia and Thailand (Chapter 3), the tensions between violence and peace in Japan and Sri Lanka (Chapter 4), the significance of land as the source of life in Australia and Melanesia (Chapter 5), the ethical values on which the economy is based in Thailand and Melanesia (Chapter 6), and the moral challenge of the refugee crisis engulfing the entire region (Chapter 7).

On this basis, we shall try to assess the religions' capacity to come to terms with the globalisation of their theologies in the wider civil society through theological cooperation and ecumenical openness (Part III), first in the form of 'collaborative' theologies (Chapter 8) and finally in a framework that is 'ecumenical' in the original meaning of the word (Chapter 9).

It is unfortunately unavoidable that this project, which tries to make comparisons among the apparently insuperable differences between the nations and cultures of the Asia-Pacific, will give the impression of being 'Western'. The approach harks back to the philosophy of the European Enlightenment with its claim to explain the world by science and bring to light the ethical foundations of humanity. If our intention is theological, however, such generalisations are necessary. Until Buddhist, Islamic and indigenous thinkers deal with these problems of comparison –

Introduction

which, as we shall see, is already happening – we will have to put up with the accusation that we are 'Westernising'.

In studying the potential of the region's societies and religions to tackle the problems of globalisation, I hope to call into question the crass secularism of Western observers and dent their complacency. What is happening to the religions in global civil society is far more interesting than the myopic secularity of Western countries would suggest.

PART 1

The Origins of Civil Society

Chapter 1: The Religious Roots of Democracy

In the social systems of the tribal cultures that Europeans somewhat condescendingly call 'traditional' or even 'primitive', there is practically no such thing as privacy. Just about everything – from marital conflicts to business deals – happens under the gaze of the community. There are sacred rituals, such as mens or womens initiation rites, which are kept secret, though these too are carried out in the name of the community, so that boys and girls may become adults and be enabled to take their place in society. Everything else – celebrating festivals, the resolution of conflicts or the decision to hunt or pursue enemies – is 'political' and happens in public.[1] The public sphere of modern societies is something quite different. It presupposes a private sphere (formerly the family, today the various forms of partnership and community), in which there is a certain level of education and political awareness, which is brought to bear in the public forum of democracy.

In this sense, Habermas speaks of "a privacy related to the public domain",[2] because it was out of the emerging private

---

1 May, John D'Arcy, "Contested Space: Alternative Models of the Public Sphere in the Asia-Pacific", Neil Brown and Robert Gascoigne, eds, *Faith in the Public Forum* (Adelaide: Australian Theological Forum, 1999), 78-108; *id.*, "Mehr als Schulung. Religiöses Lernen als Identitätsstiftung im Südpazifik", Engelbert Groß and Klaus König, eds, *Religiöses Lernen der Kirchen im globalen Dialog. Weltweit akute Herausforderungen und Praxis einer Weggemeinschaft für Eine-Welt-Religionspädagogik* (Münster-Hamburg-London: LIT Verlag, 2000), 107-121; *id.*, "Initiation, Initiationsverlust und Initiationsersatz im Südpazifik", Thomas Schreijäck, ed., *Menschwerden im Kulturwandel. Kontexte kultureller Identität als Wegmarken interkultureller Kompetenz* (Luzern: Edition Exodus, 1999), 456-471.

2 "[E]ine publikumsbezogene Privatheit", Habermas, Jürgen, *Strukturwandel der Öffentlichkeit* (Frankfurt: Suhrkamp, 1990, orig. 1962), 17, 107. See also Brewer, John D., "The Limits of Politics in Northern Ireland's Peace Process", John O'Grady, Cathy Higgins und Jude Lal Fernando, eds, *Mining Truths: Festschrift in Honour of Geraldine Smyth OP – Ecumenical Theologian and Peacebuilder* (St.

sphere of educated and articulate (and male and property-owning) citizens that the public sphere took shape in Europe as a *political* force capable of criticising and counterbalancing the inherited power of the aristocracy.[3] The public sphere is thus a fundamental presupposition of the Enlightenment and the emancipation it inspired. Its existence did not always bring about democratic freedoms, as the political chaos of Weimar Germany and that country's subsequent problems with authoritarian and totalitarian regimes show. Privacy, in the age of electronic communication and surveillance, is in the process of becoming the expensive privilege of an elite, while others are exposed to the intrusions of advertising, security forces, hackers or merely the inquisitive, and social media bypass the established channels of public communication.

Here, we wish to pursue the possibility that civil society could become global, but as a prelude to this it will be necessary to scrutinise the accepted understanding of democracy as something that originated in Greek antiquity but only came fully into its own during the European Enlightenment (1.1). This will help us assess the role of the public sphere in the emergence of democracy in societies outside Europe (1.2), which will be our touchstone as we investigate the emergence of global civil society (1.3).

1.1 Origins and Transformations of Civil Society

One of the leading advocates of global civil society is the Australian political scientist John Keane.[4] His research reveals that there

---

Ottilien: EOS Verlag, 2015), 185-201, esp. 187-189 on the disappearance of the distinction between public and private, political and social.

3   Habermas, *Öffentlichkeit*, Chapter IV, in which he traces the evolution of the notion of 'public opinion' through the works of Hobbes, Rousseau, Locke, Kant, Hegel, Marx, Mill and Tocquville.

4   Keane, John, *Global Civil Society?* (Cambridge: Cambridge University Press, 2003); see also Kaldor, Mary, *Global Civil Society: An Answer to War* (Cambridge: Polity Press, 2003).

were many forms of democratic public life which were not only present long before the assemblies of the Pnyx and the Agora in ancient Athens, but were found throughout the Greek islands as far back as ancient Mycenae. Not only that: it is more than probable that the inspiration for these lawmaking assemblies came from Mesopotamia, that is, present-day Syria and Iraq, possibly via Persia.

In ancient India, at the time of the Buddha around 500 BCE, there were so-called 'republics' with collective leadership, from one of which Gautama was descended as the son of a 'prince' or ruler. In all such cases, the basic principle was that the *demos* – the people (generally restricted to male heads of families and property owners) – had the right to govern itself. Where such *demokratia* was taken literally in the sense that the common people as distinct from privileged elites had the final say in affairs of state, it was often condemned as 'mob rule', as in Book VIII of Plato's *Republic*. Nevertheless, this 'assembly democracy', as Keane calls it, was found throughout the ancient world and arose very early.[5]

From this one can already conclude that "democracies require public spaces",[6] but it is equally true that "except for a tiny handful of cases democracy has never been built democratically".[7] It also becomes apparent that "no democracy is an island unto itself": the Arcadian League (370 BCE) could justly be called a democracy of democracies,[8] but in Athens military success at Marathon and Salamis and in the Delian League meant that

---

[5] Keane, John, *The Life and Death of Democracy* (London-Sydney-New York-Toronto: Pocket Books [Simon and Schuster], 2009), 1-62. Keane traces assembly democracy as far back as Byblos around 1100 BCE, 106-107, and he points out that kings in Mesopotamia did not see themselves as 'oriental despots', but as servants of the gods in *their* assembly, 110-111.

[6] Keane, *Democracy*, 14.

[7] Keane, *Democracy*, 4.

[8] Keane, *Democracy*, 64, 96.

building up the army and navy took priority, resulting in the loss of civil liberties and eventually the *hubris* of imperial domination.[9] This was "non-secular democracy" for which freedom was a divine gift; it was direct democracy in which there were no parties, no 'representatives': in the assembly (*ekklesia*) all were equal before the law (*isonomia*), but in this equality there was the potential for unpredictability.[10] More important for us, however, is that these findings unmask the "dogma of Western democracy" as an orientalist prejudice.[11] These precursors of modern democracy were the result of interchange with the East.

Not only that: after the virtual disappearance of assembly democracy with the decline of the Roman Empire, it was revived by Islam. The absolute transcendence of Allah was the basis of a truly universal ethic, which even extended to the protection of plants and animals. Islam was a religion of traders, relying on partnership rather than class warfare. The rise of the Caliphs under the Umayyads and Abbasids suffocated democratic tendencies, but "[t]he growth of a swathe of social institutions that Muslim and other scholars later called 'civil society' (*jamaa'i-madani*) was unknown to Greeks, Phoenicians and the peoples of Syria-Mesopotamia".[12] An example that has endured till today is the *waqf*, a charitable endowment intended to alleviate poverty and promote the just distribution of wealth, thus helping to curb the excesses of authoritarian regimes. "The resulting social ties were typically multiple and fluid and dynamic", for Muslim society was "simultaneously religious and social and political … Islam rolled law, government and politics into one packet. All law was

---

9   Keane, *Democracy*, 71-72.
10   Keane, *Democracy*, 15, 36-38, 53-54.
11   Keane, *Democracy*, 102-103.
12   Keane, *Democracy*, 133, see 128-132.

seen to be of divine origin".[13] The first scholar to describe this social and political order as 'democracy' (*al-madina al-jamaiyya*) was al-Farabi (ca. 870-950 CE); Tamiyya (1263-1328) advocated consultative assemblies; the Mu'tazilites criticised unaccountable authority.

It is, therefore, no exaggeration to say that "Islam played a fundamental role in the renaissance and redefinition of democracy" in that it held to "the principle that government is only ever legitimate when it has been sanctioned by the active consent of the representatives chosen by the governed themselves".[14] The relevance of these observations will become apparent when we turn to examine present-day Islamic societies in Part II.

1.2 Democracy and Civil Society

An essential component of stable public life is civility (from Lat. *civis*, 'citizen'), based on respect for others. Civility makes or enables the development of non-violent forms of behaviour which make it possible to mediate conflicts of interest by 'the force of the better argument' (Habermas) rather than force of arms. In traditional societies, as was once said to me in Indonesia, there are no losers. After long and free discussions, the achievement of consensus occurs when the designated head of the community (in Melanesia, the 'big man', *bikman*; in Aboriginal Australia, the tribal elder) announces agreement and gives it the force of authority.

In democratic societies, there is an adversarial system culminating in a vote (in parliament) or verdict (in court), which is recognised even by those who lose as an attempt to establish the truth and enact justice. Whole governments are voted out and

---

13   Keane, *Democracy*, 135, 141, 144.
14   Keane, *Democracy*, 145-152, 154-155.

replaced; the highest offices are subject to fresh elections after a statutory period. These arrangements presuppose a high degree of information and awareness. It must be possible to form one's own opinion without undue pressure. Although we know that, as a rule, political propaganda influences voters, ideally citizens before an election and jury members in a trial make their judgments on the basis of the facts, which presupposes concepts such as 'objectivity' and 'truth'. For this reason, one would think, it is as difficult to uphold freedom of opinion and the independence of the judiciary in societies whose religious and cultural traditions are pronouncedly communal as it is in those governed by authoritarian regimes.

Yet we increasingly observe that these very concepts are being devalued in the democracies of the West by slogans such as 'post-truth', 'fake news' and 'alternative facts'. The undermining of the priority of truth and with it the possibility of trust is fatal to democracy. In this regard, George Orwell's novel *Nineteen Eighty-four*, first published in 1949, with its Newspeak overseen by the Ministry of Truth, is eerily prophetic. Suffice it to say that in the Asia-Pacific, most societies fall roughly in the middle of a scale ranging from 'closed' to 'open', from 'collective' to 'individualistic'.

The exercise of democratic freedoms naturally requires a certain degree of prosperity and economic equality. The separation of powers, the franchise, health care, education and, not least, the rights of women, mean that citizens, relatively unburdened by feelings of injustice, need or ideological prejudice, can decide freely. For those who, like me, have always lived in more or less functioning democracies, all this may seem taken for granted. For others, such as the citizens of South Africa, East Timor or Myanmar, who experience free elections for the very first time, it is anything but; we need only take note of the extraordinary efforts they make, often in the face of real dangers, to exercise their vote. It is all the more remarkable – not to say ominous – that democratic freedoms in many states, especially those stemming from former colonies, but also in China or Russia, are positively loathed by those in power – though not necessarily by the people at large – and that people, either as individuals or organised in religiously inspired movements, seem afraid of freedom and despise candidates who are seen as 'liberal' or 'secular', as was the case in Algeria and still is in Egypt.

Indeed, the granting of democratic freedoms is seen as some kind of lunacy or weakness. Ethnic or religious loyalties are sometimes too strong to allow experiments with the public competition of opposing parties. In Western eyes, this is all the more difficult to understand in that people then put themselves in the hands of ambitious and corrupt elites. It is cause for concern that religions often play an important part in such situations. One of the main objects of the present study is to understand this better.

According to Hegel, civil society mediates between the private sphere of the family and the public sphere of the state.[15] It even has the role of protecting citizens from the state, for in a democracy the state may not arrogate to itself total control or unrestricted power. The personal freedoms and political rights of the citizens are values in themselves, which may not be interfered with. But for reasons we have yet to investigate, these values are regarded as 'Western' with an afterglow of 'Christian', and for this reason alone they are problematic in cultures which have been influenced by other religious traditions such as Buddhism and Islam in the course of a painful experience of colonialism. We are perhaps not sufficiently aware that the free space of 'liberal' democracy

---

15 Kaldor, Mary, "The Idea of Global Civil Society", *International Affairs* 79/3 (2003), 583-593, 584.

is restricted to a relatively small number of nation states, which together make up 'the West' or 'the free world'. Elsewhere, often enough, the military, monarchs or dictators enjoy unfettered power. There are, naturally, a number of genuinely democratic nations in the so-called Third World, which only achieved a degree of independence in the twentieth century; Papua New Guinea is a lively and colourful example. There are said to be between 114 and 119 democracies in the world, making up about sixty per cent of states, but since 2000, some 25 democratic states have collapsed.[16]

The modern history of India, as we shall see, throws into doubt many aspects of democracy which Westerners take for granted. It is difficult to deny that in many cases the institutions of democracy have been imposed on non-Western cultures, which may well have developed in quite different directions if they had been allowed to evolve their own ways of building consensus. The 'civic space' of Western societies was reproduced without regard for the 'sacral space' of peoples whose organic development was deeply influenced by religion. Sometimes this succeeds (India, South Korea, Japan), sometimes not (China, Cambodia, Vietnam); in other cases (Thailand, Indonesia, Sri Lanka), compromises are reached which are not entirely stable, whereas yet others (Singapore, Malaysia) understand themselves as democracies, but with different – authoritarian and ethnic – priorities.

Parliaments are not necessarily democratic; democracies are not necessarily liberal.[17] Those who inspired and promoted the construction of modern democracies, whether in Europe or America, were often more republican than democratic; some were emphatically anti-democratic. The American founding fathers were afraid of mob rule and regarded the idea of representative

---

[16] Friedman, Thomas, "Democracy Worldwide Goes Deeper into Recession", *The Age* (Melbourne), 22/2/2015.

[17] Keane, *Democracy*, 161-162, 181.

democracy as problematic.[18] This, of course, is the specifically European form of democracy. It took shape in the course of a long and complex development in the Middle Ages in which the Christian church played a considerable role.

The idea of an 'office holder' was part of the church's Roman heritage. Those who held office 're-presented' the faithful of their local churches at the universal or regional councils. In the ferment surrounding the Council of Constance (1414), this principle of 'conciliarity', as it came to be called at the time of the Second Vatican Council, took the form of a theory of 'conciliarism', according, to which the council, in a situation in which three rival pretenders to the papal office sought to outmanoeuvre one another, possessed the authority to exercise the papal office and appoint a pope. After the crisis had passed, the conciliarists almost succeeded in perpetuating the status of the council alongside or even above the authority of the pope.

This precedent became a turning point in the development of parliamentary democracy. Thus "the early Christian church in effect functioned as a bridge that led from the world of ancient assemblies to the modern world of representation".[19] The Reformers, too, though not exactly democratically minded, made the concept of covenant the basis of citizens' resistance to unjust governments – in their case, the papists – thereby helping to prepare the ground for the freedoms of civil society.[20] "The Covenant of 1557 constitutes a climax in the development of the

---

18   Keane, *Democracy*, 275.
19   Keane, *Democracy*, 219; cf. 219-226. See also May, John D'Arcy, "Vorbereitende Überlegungen zu einer Konsenstheorie der Konziliarität", *Una Sancta* 32 (1977), 94-104; Tierney, Brian, *Foundations of the Conciliar Theory: The Contribution of the Medieval Canonists from Gratian to the Great Schism* (Cambridge: Cambridge University Press, 1955); Bäumer, Remigius, ed., *Die Entwicklung des Konziliarismus. Werden und Nachwirkung der konziliaren Idee* (Darmstadt: Wissenschaftliche Buchgesellschaft, 1976).
20   Keane, *Democracy*, 232-240.

Scottish Reformation".[21] The Scottish Protestants, inspired by Calvin and powerfully influenced by John Knox, moved towards a form of church government in which there was no supreme head, the clergy were all equal, and the laity had a decisive role through the Kirk Session and the General Assembly.

This form of church organisation was tempered in the struggle with King James VI (1567-1625), who favoured an episcopal system which he could control. The Calvinists, under Andrew Melville, insisted on the presbyterial form of a 'pure church' (hence the name 'Puritans'). "They gave themselves a democratic church organisation and thus became Presbyterians ... Their idea of an autonomous congregation under Christ as its unique head contributed substantially to the American notion of democracy as the political form of government most in accord with God's will".[22] It is thus no surprise that it was the Puritan preachers rather than European liberals who inspired the independence of the American colonies and the democratic elements in the republican constitution.[23] It is nonetheless undeniable that as a reaction to the European wars of religion and the American civil war the liberal ideals of tolerance, freedom of opinion and freedom of religion became the cornerstones of representative parliamentary democracy.

---

21   Iserloh, Erwin, "Europe under the Sign of Confessional Pluralism", Erwin Iserloh, Josef Glazik, Hubert Jedin, eds, *Reformation and Counter Reformation, History of the Church, Vol. V* (London: Burns & Oates, 1980), 410-419, 412.

22   Iserloh, "Confessional Pluralism", 419. In Ireland I used to say – only in private! – that the Presbyterians, because of their rigorous egalitarianism and direct elections, were the real Republicans.

23   Hoye, William J., *Demokratie und Christentum. Die christliche Verantwortung für demokratische Prinzipien* (Münster: Aschendorff, 1999), Chapter III.

1.3 From Religious to Political Pluralism

At the heart of the Enlightenment heritage lies freedom of religion. It was the first and most fundamental freedom that the *Treaty of Westphalia* (1648) established as the culmination of decades of struggle between Catholic and Protestant princes and the popes and prelates who tried to salvage the Counter-Reformation and enact the reforms demanded by the Council of Trent (1545-1553). It amounted to a reluctant acknowledgment of the reality of religious pluralism as the enduring legacy of the Reformation by providing for sovereign nation states of different Christian confessions in a kind of balance of power. The resulting conception of religious freedom formed the basis of both religious and political pluralism, eventually not only *between* but *within* nation states, and not just among Christian confessions but, in the course of time, among fundamentally different non-native religious communities.[24]

But the basic component of this new order in Europe – and, in the course of colonisation, beyond its shores – remained the sovereign, independent, territorial nation state. Only today is this political entity, and therewith the concept of 'international relations', beginning to be questioned as the framework for international peace. National governments increasingly prove to be powerless against the attempts of multinational corporations to claim priority over national laws for their right to trade freely and move their profits to wherever they can evade tax, not to mention arms deals, copyright infringements, drug smuggling, people trafficking and other ways of showing contempt for national sovereignty.

These abuses make more plausible the idea of global governance (not a global government!) but the legal and political

---

24 May, John D'Arcy, "God in Public: The Religions in Pluralist Societies", *Bijdragen: International Journal in Philosophy and Theology* 64/3 (2003), 249-264.

structures for its implementation are lacking. There is also talk of a 'democracy of democracies',[25] which would relativise the sovereignty of nation states, though this has proved so controversial in Europe that it has provided the pretext for Brexit, Britain's exit from the European Union. These developments, together with electronic communications media, ease of travel and multinational trade relations, could be the precursors of a widening of civil society over the heads of nation states. Hence the thesis of an emerging *global* civil society, which need not mean, however, that the West's political structures and behavioural norms are simply extended to the rest of the world. Rather, civil society appears to spring up and flourish spontaneously, wherever there is a minimum of free space and media of communication, despite the repression imposed by insecure governments (such as China, Russia and other authoritarian states). It takes on the cultural colouring of its environment, and in many cases it is quite informally religious.

The religions do not remain untouched by this phenomenon of ever-widening communication. They, too, become increasingly aware of one another, and must learn to get along with one another in situations they have never encountered in their countries of origin. The idea that democracy and hence civil society must be 'secular' is a Western construct. It stems from the fact that, in the post-Reformation period, the power of the churches had to be broken if rights were to be established and the sciences were to flourish. Essential to this was the autonomy of the individual, entailing the right to private property and the exercise of freedom, as Kant and Mill insisted. We may expect similar processes of

---

[25] Held, David, "Democracy: From City-states to a Cosmopolitan Order?", *id.*, ed., *Prospects for Democracy: North, South, East, West* (Cambridge: Polity Press, 1993), 13-52; Falk, Richard, "Humane Governance for the World: Reviving the Quest", Rorden Wilkinson, ed., *The Global Governance Reader* (London/New York: Routledge, 2005), 105-119; Scholte, Jan Aart, "Civil Society and Democracy in Global Governance", *ibid.*, 322-340.

emancipation to play out in Islamic societies and among Muslims in the West.

But there are other cultural conditions under which concepts like 'rights' and 'freedoms' are alien and threatening.[26] Duty and responsibility to the community have a much higher status in such societies. In different ways, this is true for the island cultures of the South Pacific (such as Papua New Guinea, Fiji, Tonga and the Micronesian states) and for the sacral kingdoms of Asia (the leader as *devaraja*, 'divine king', in Indonesia; the king as *bodhisattva*, 'great being' on the path to enlightenment, in Thailand; the emperor as *kami*, 'supernatural power', in Japan).

In such contexts, 'land' is not simply an objective entity, something that can be quantified and offered for sale (which does not prevent corrupt politicians and business people from gaining possession of fertile land and making a profit out of its resources). Land is rather the 'place' – in Aboriginal Australia 'country' – which gives life and in which one is culturally rooted. An individualistic understanding of law that is not orientated to land and community is completely out of place in such contexts.

In the immigrant quarters of Western cities, however, and throughout the global public sphere, the encounter with ideas such as freedom of movement and opinion is unavoidable, and for the alienated and exploited migrants and refugees who populate these living spaces it is understandable that such ideas awaken feelings of envy or even hatred. These, reinforced by religious ideologies such as radical Islamism, become the motivation for terrorist attacks that lash out at the 'good life' paraded before them, which can come to

---

26   May, John D'Arcy, "Human Rights as Land Rights in the Pacific", *Pacifica: Australian Theological Studies* 6 (1993), 61-80; *id.* and Linda Hogan, "Constructing the Human: Dignity in Interreligious Dialogue", Regina Ammicht-Quinn, Maureen Junker-Kenny and Elsa Tamez, eds, *The Discourse of Human Dignity* (London: SCM, *Concilium* 2003/2), 78-89.

appear as the embodiment of evil. When migrants or refugees, who have lived at home in a taken for granted religious milieu accepted by all, find themselves as members of despised minorities, their emotional alienation is intensified. The recruitment of Western volunteers for Islamic State can be partially explained in this way, as can attacks by Islamic youths who, to all appearances, are at home in Western societies.

But not only indigenous traditions and social minorities are affected by such conditions: the so-called world religions, too, must come to terms with the loss of the social standing they have enjoyed since ancient times. The function of religion is changing, both in pluralistic societies and in the global public sphere. The religions may be compared with one another, they must justify themselves in public, and they have to accept diminishing numbers of adherents. Religion is being de-regulated and de-privatised; it is *one* factor among others playing a role in a much wider and more uncomfortable public arena. No religion defines 'the whole' anymore; other religions and especially the sciences compete with them in this role.[27] The religions are reduced to sub-systems within a larger whole, which they no longer define. This experience is traumatic for them, but also stimulating, in a certain analogy to the area of culture (world literature, world music).

Global civil society presupposes a public sphere which potentially includes the whole of humanity. It is no longer physically located within the heavily guarded borders of particular territories, but on planet earth. It is a forum for debate about problems that are common to all, from environmental pollution and global warming to economic or political refugees and ethnic-

---

27   Beyer, Peter, *Religions in Global Society* (London and New York: Routledge, 2006); Hollenbach, David, *The Global Face of Public Faith: Politics, Human Rights, and Christian Ethics* (Washington, DC: Georgetown University Press, 2003).

religious conflicts. There are, of course, a number of overarching international institutions – UNO, EU, NATO, ASEAN – but all in their different ways are problematic and ineffectual. The religions, too, have their world organisations: the Vatican, the World Council of Churches, the Islamic and Buddhist world congresses, the World Conference of Religions for Peace, the World Parliament of Religions, the United Religions Initiative etc. The newly rediscovered 'catholicity' of the Christian church, the worldwide Islamic *ummah* (community) and the Buddhist *sangha* (the Order in the widest sense) are examples of truly universal consensus communities at a deeper level.

But in their own ways, these supra-national structures are also problematic: in addition to their internal problems with division and dissent, they lack the credibility to assert themselves in the public square, especially in a global context. The global public sphere that is presently taking shape needs to be structured and made functional; but how? The religions do not simply inhabit this new, putatively neutral space alongside others: they resonate through it, fill it with content, create the issues that enliven it. The following study will be concerned with the ways in which they might overcome their exclusivist and fundamentalist animosities and take advantage of the global public sphere to move closer together.

Chapter 2: Globalisation and Westernisation

If we are right in assuming that civil society is generally seen as both a precondition and a product of the European Enlightenment, so that it is understood to be necessarily secular, liberal and pluralistic, then it is not surprising that in many other cultural contexts civil society is associated with *Western* modernity. For those who have never experienced liberty, equality and fraternity, the freedoms implied by civil society can be irresistibly attractive; but often this attraction is overshadowed by the fear that tried and trusted existing ways of ordering society will be dismantled.

The guaranteed freedoms on which civil society depends were, for the most part, bitterly fought for, often against the resistance of churches (we may think of the determined efforts of the Roman Catholic Church to defend itself against modernity), the religions (for example in the Islamic countries of the Arab world), or authoritarian ideologies (the suppression of human rights in China, Turkey or Myanmar).

Western modernity, despite the fact that its products are strongly desirable, is suspect: it connotes atheism, immorality, secularity, as can be seen in the electoral defeats of 'secular' parties in Algeria or Egypt. This is the source of the hatred of democracy that seems so irrational to Europeans, the rejection of civil rights, the resistance to Western education (in Nigeria *boko haram* means precisely this: Western education prohibited). The personal autonomy and bodily integrity of the individual, adequate health care and the freedom to choose one's partner are denied or threatened in such contexts. Why? What does 'Western' actually mean?[1] We need to investigate these matters (2.1). This suggests

---

1   An original interpretation may be found in Dussel, Enrique, *Von der Erfindung Amerikas zur Entdeckung des Anderen* (Düsseldorf: Patmos, 1993

the further question whether there are non-Western versions of civil society and hence avenues to democracy in quite different cultural contexts (2.2). Only then can we begin to explain what globalisation means for the religions (2.3).

2.1 'Why do they hate us so much?'

This is the question that perplexed Americans are said to have asked themselves after the attacks of 11 September 2001. The fact that in many parts of the world the West has become the object of envy and hatred does indeed raise serious questions. In the Islamic world, 'Roman' implied European Christian influence (the *rumi* were in fact the peoples of the Eastern Roman Empire; the crusaders, coming from further west, were known as 'Franks'). For the Buddhist countries of Southeast Asia as for India, China and Japan, the term 'European', with its Christian connotations, was correspondingly threatening (Japan, as is well known, closed itself against European influence for 200 years, while China was exploited and humiliated by European mercantile powers, culminating in the infamous Opium Wars).

'The West' is the product of the fusion of Greco-Roman cultural values and the biblical Jewish heritage in medieval 'Christendom'. Here, not unlike the Islamic Caliphate,[2] church and society formed a unified polity; the struggles between throne and altar, emperor and pope played out within this unquestioned framework. The external threats – from the Muslims in the south,

---

= Theologie Interkulturell 6), 189-192, where he develops twelve different meanings of the terms 'Europe', 'the West', 'modernity' and 'late capitalism'; see also 193-198 on the Eurocentric as opposed to a 'trans-modern' paradigm of modernity.

2 See Nagel, Tilman, *Staat und Glaubensgemeinschaft im Islam. Geschichte der politischen Ordnungsvorstellungen der Muslime. Band I: Von den Anfängen bis ins 13. Jahrhundert* (Zürich-München: Artemis, 1981).

the Vikings in the north and the Tartars in the east – had the effect of stabilising the unity of the Western part of the former Roman Empire (the East had been definitively separated from Rome in 1054).

The rise of the Eastern Orthodox churches, the crusades and the voyages of discovery, especially those embarked on by Columbus since 1492, contributed to this. The latter coincided with the expulsion of the Muslims and Jews from Spain, united under the Catholic monarchs Ferdinand and Isabella. These developments, which may fairly be said to mark the beginning of modernity, made the West aware of itself as a cultural and political entity,[3] reinforced by the Reformation and the ensuing Wars of Religion, the rediscovery of the cultures of antiquity in the Renaissance and the assertion of the autonomy of the individual and the primacy of reason in the Enlightenment.

Western Europe thus became a dynamic historical power which 'discovered' (for itself), colonised and transformed much of the rest of the world. In view of this history of conquest and exploitation, it is understandable that the West, despite the desirability of its inventions and consumer goods, awakens resentment in the peoples of its former colonies. It may even be said to have *created* these extra-European cultures and constructed them as its 'others',[4] repressing and humiliating them in the process, even if at the same time it modernised and energised them, liberating them to rediscover themselves and regain their

---

[3] Collins, Paul, *The Birth of the West: Rome, Germany, France, and the Creation of Europe in the Tenth Century* (New York: Public Affairs, 2013), traces the formation of what we now call Western Europe much further back, to the order that gradually emerged from the chaos of the early tenth century, imposed largely by the vigour and vision of the three German Ottos, I-III.

[4] Said, Edward, *Orientalism: Western Conceptions of the Orient* (London: Penguin, 1991, orig. 1978); *id.*, *Culture and Imperialism* (London: Vintage, 1994).

autonomy. It was to be expected that they would then claim the right to go their own ways, not least in matters of governance and political structure.[5]

Along with this goes the process generally known today as 'secularisation'. The term stems from the dissolution of the monasteries and the forced laicisation of the monks and nuns in the course of the Reformation. In modern times, however, partly as a result of confessional divisions and the rise of humanism, it means the autonomy of the world as demonstrated by the natural sciences, *etsi deus non daretur* ('as if there were no God'). The result was not only secularisation as a new sensibility, but secularism, an ideology which, like French *laïcité*, banned everything religious from the public sphere and was reinforced by scientism, which made the methods of the natural sciences the criterion for all knowledge, entrenching the dualism formulated by Descartes. Secularism brought the human to the fore, but it also reduced it to an 'exclusive humanism'.[6]

The profundity of this change, "which takes us from a society in which it was virtually impossible not to believe in God, to one in which faith, even for the staunchest believer, is one human possibility among others",[7] is not always grasped by contemporaries with little knowledge of what the religions once were and, in many ways, still are. As we have already seen, this intellectual development coincided with the breakthrough to democratic

---

[5] May, John D'Arcy, "Der Osten des Westens. Europa vor der Herausforderung des interreligiösen Dialogs", *Ost-West. Europäische Perspektiven* 3 (2002), 243-253; *id.*, "Europe's God: Liberator or Oppressor? The Postcolonial Mediation of Transcendence", Norbert Hintersteiner, ed., *Naming and Thinking God in Europe Today: Theology in Global Dialogue* (Amsterdam and New York: Editions Rodopi, 2007), 69-92.

[6] This whole development has been described in masterly fashion by Taylor, Charles, *A Secular Age* (Cambridge, Mass. & London: The Belknap Press of Harvard University Press, 2007).

[7] Taylor, *Secular Age*, 3.

forms of government by a gradual evolution of parliamentary democracy in Great Britain and explosive revolutions in France and North America. The resulting conjunction of intellectual and religious pluralism with the heightened economic conflicts occasioned by colonialism occurred in the 'neutral' framework of liberality and tolerance.

This by no means implies that these new types of social order did not produce their own ideological divisions and social stratifications. Alexis de Tocqueville, a French aristocrat of liberal convictions, while acknowledging the new possibilities opened up for social and political life by the emerging American democracy, was dismayed by tendencies he did not hesitate to call the collective tyranny of the majority and the slavery of public opinion; he concludes with a critique of democratic absolutism as a menace to freedom.[8]

In conscious continuity with the astute sociological analyses of Tocqueville, Robert Bellah and his associates have delved deeper into the dynamics of democratic evolution in American society.[9] Their title, *Habits of the Heart*, is Tocqueville's term for what today would be called 'mores', the meanings and values implicit in socially sanctioned ways of behaving.[10] Taking up Tocqueville's central theme "that a variety of active civic organizations are the key to American democracy", for they "mediate between the individual and the centralized state, providing forums in which opinion can be publicly and intelligently shaped", the authors examine what we have been calling 'civil society'.[11] Their research brings into

---

8   Tocqueville, Alexis de, *De la Démocratie en Amérique* (Paris: Union Générale, 1963), Book I (1835), Chapter 15; Book II (1840), Chapter 28.
9   Bellah, Robert N., Richard Madsen, William M. Sullivan, Ann Swidler, and Steven M. Tipton, *Habits of the Heart: Individualism and Commitment in American Life* (New York et al.: Harper & Row, 1986).
10   Bellah et al., *Habits of the Heart*, 37.
11   Bellah et al., *Habits of the Heart*, 38.

focus what Tocqueville was one of the first to call 'individualism', the tendency of citizens in open societies to keep their distance from inherited forms of behaviour and fall back on their own moral and psychological resources. The resulting tensions in the lives of many of their interview subjects make the authors "wonder if psychological sophistication has not been bought at the price of moral impoverishment".[12]

Tocqueville was in no doubt that this individualism "was strangely compatible with conformism".[13] Individualism's "primary emphasis on self-reliance has led to the notion of pure, undetermined choice, free of tradition, obligation, or commitment, as the essence of the self".[14] But the self does not emerge out of nothing; it can only subsist in what the Bellah team call 'communities of memory', so that "we live somewhere between the empty and the constituted self".[15] A variation on this theme is that "in an individualistic culture that highly values diversity and 'pluralism', it is consensus that is appreciated and the conflict of interests that is suspect".[16] We shall need to return to these observations when we come to consider the dynamics that develop when an individualistic ethos based on pluralism and antagonistic viewpoints is introduced into societies that have only ever known a profound mythico-religious consensus, reflected in centralised and unitary systems of government.

More recently, those who had proclaimed that secularisation was the innate tendency of modernising societies have been having second thoughts, and others point to the return of religion in

---

12   Bellah *et al.*, *Habits of the Heart*, 139.
13   Bellah *et al.*, *Habits of the Heart*, 147; see the whole of Chapter 6 on individualism.
14   Bellah *et al.*, *Habits of the Heart*, 152.
15   Bellah *et al.*, *Habits of the Heart*, 154; see 152-162.
16   Bellah *et al.*, *Habits of the Heart*, 203.

politics and political science.[17] We see an exodus of religion from traditional institutions to become free-floating in the pluralism and multiculturalism of open societies, while much sought-after 'spirituality' is marketed as a lifestyle product. These developments are undergoing a further transformation in the course of what is not uncontroversially known as 'globalisation'.

The phenomenon is not entirely new; in antiquity, too, there were world empires (China, India, Persia, Rome). But industrialisation and the new forms of transport it stimulated, together with electronic communications media, which allow social relations and economic transactions to take place in real time, have no parallel in the whole of history, though we should remember that millions of human beings still have no access to electricity, let alone the Internet, and their travels are likely to be on trucks and leaky boats as they try to escape intolerable violence and poverty.

For this very reason, globalisation has acquired a negative connotation: it is widely understood to mean even more sophisticated ways of exploiting labour, destroying the environment and enriching the privileged.[18] But in and of itself globalisation is a purely formal concept, prompting the question: globalisation of what? The arms trade and drug smuggling have also been globalised, but so too have scientific research, cultural exchange, friendship networks and social relations. It is, therefore, to be expected that the religions are caught up in this process of

---

17 Berger, Peter, *The Desecularization of the World: Resurgent Religion and World Politics* (Washington: Ethics and Public Policy Center; Grand Rapids: Eerdmans, 1999); Casanova, José, *Public Religions in the Modern World* (Chicago: University of Chicago Press, 1994); Petito, Fabio, und Pavlos Hatzopoulos, eds, *Religion in International Relations: The Return from Exile* (New York: Palgrave Macmillan, 2003).

18 Stiglitz, Joseph, *Globalization and its Discontents* (New York: Norton, 2002); see Boff, Leonardo, *Global Civilization: Challenges to Society and Christianity* (London/Oakville: Equinox, 2005, orig. 2003).

globalisation. It will be one of the main purposes of this study to investigate the reciprocal effects of globalisation on the religions and vice-versa, with special regard to the Asia-Pacific region. If a global civil society is indeed emerging, it will not be exclusively 'Western'; other variants of civil society will have their own parts to play.

2.2   Civil Society in Non-Western Contexts

We have already put down one marker for the present situation: *politically*, the imposition of Western democratic structures within artificially created state boundaries on societies with other cultural traditions is over (as the colonial history of China, the disastrous experiments in Iraq, Afghanistan and Egypt, and many examples in Africa demonstrate); *religiously* the discrediting of indigenous cultures as 'pagan', 'irreligious' or even 'immoral' in order to justify forced Christianisation (although this is still practised by North American fundamentalists, Latin American Pentecostals, Korean missionaries and African wealth-and-prosperity churches) is also, or should be, a thing of the past, as is Islamisation (still prevalent in Indonesia, especially West Papua, throughout the Middle East and Africa, and in southern Thailand and the Philippines).

These tendencies can be seen in a certain sense as symptoms of globalisation: peoples who are repelled by the Western prosperity from which they are shut out want to be truly themselves, sure of their identity and independent, and they reach back to cultural and religious traditions that promise a spiritual renewal *against* the West. In this way, new forms of cultural autonomy, religious revival and not least political self-determination come about; but they bear the strong –Western – imprint of political nationalism and religious fundamentalism.

The results are not always pretty: think of the sorry failure of the 'Arab Spring' in Libya or Egypt and especially in Syria, where a ruler is prepared to see his country destroyed rather than give up power; the almost insuperable difficulties confronting the democratisation of Myanmar, Laos, Cambodia and Vietnam; Indonesia's efforts to maintain national unity in the face of struggles for autonomy or liberation in East Timor, Aceh and West Papua. The barbaric terror unleashed by the so-called Islamic State is perhaps the most fundamental and explicit challenge to the West we have yet seen, though a movement based on such manifest duplicity and thuggery could not last long as a territorial state. From an Asia-Pacific point of view, however, the unstoppable rise of China and the rapid modernisation of India are possibly even more threatening, because they cause seismic power shifts implicating American allies like Japan, South Korea or Australia.

The example of India is particularly instructive in this regard. No one really foresaw that in this huge country with numerous languages, cultures and religions, suffocating poverty and widespread illiteracy, a Westminster-style democracy could survive. Yet despite the bloody excesses that accompanied the separation of Muslim Pakistan from the newly independent Hindu state of India and the assassination of Gandhi by a Hindu nationalist, the largest functioning democracy in the world took shape on Indian soil.

Gandhi, "a man of civil society"[19] who had led the largely peaceful liberation struggle against the British, was not political in the conventional sense. He advocated village republics rather than the institutions of representative democracy. It was Jawaharlal Nehru, the first prime minister, who led the way to a democratic future. It was he who introduced a specifically Indian form of

---

19   Keane, *Democracy*, 597.

secularity on the basis of "a principled even-handedness"[20] which included all religions and excluded every type of communalism (the Indian variety of fundamentalism). His models were neither French nor American. Nehru mistrusted the great powers and supported the non-aligned movement. He advocated five principles (*Panchsheel*) of a democratic world order:

1. Non-aggression
2. Peaceful co-existence
3. Sovereignty of states
4. Non-interference in their domestic affairs
5. Equality among states and peoples.[21]

When the ruling Congress Party under Indira Gandhi became increasingly autocratic, there was an eruption of protest from civil society, to which the government responded with a 'State of Emergency'. But Gandhi – in classic democratic fashion – was voted out of office. The casteless *Dalits*, the poorest of the poor, participated in the elections in greater numbers than before.[22] More recently, the unimaginably corrupt former prime minister of Malaysia, Najib Razak, was voted out of office in May 2018, to be replaced by his now 92 year old predecessor, Mahatir Mohammed, who stood for election with the express purpose of getting rid of Najib and paving the way for the longsuffering Anwar Ibrahim, jailed by both Mahatir and Najib in the past for his resolute opposition to their authoritarianism. Democracy in Asian countries, though under strain, is far from dead.

Two world wars all but extinguished representative democracy in Europe. The independence of former colonies, foremost among

---

20   Keane, *Democracy*, 602.
21   Keane, *Democracy*, 602-611.
22   Keane, *Democracy*, 618, 624.

them India, brought about a rebirth of democracy, albeit in a new form which had repercussions for democracy in the West, because it involved civil society in the political process in novel ways. Keane calls this 'monitory democracy', in which civil society is alert to abuses of state power and calls the powerful to account. This amounts to nothing less than "the 'indigenisation' of democracy – its embedding and mutation in contexts where formerly it was a stranger".[23]

Asian countries such as Japan, Taiwan and Indonesia became democratic for the first time ever, but not on the Western pattern. Not the competition of parties but national unity had priority. Noting the victories of 'people power' over totalitarian or authoritarian regimes, Samuel Huntington proclaimed a 'Third Wave' of democratisation, and Francis Fukuyama announced the definitive triumph of Western liberalism as the 'End of History'.[24] What we observe, on the contrary, is that democracies are in a position to defend themselves against abuses of power and attempts to exploit their weaknesses. What would once have remained secret now becomes public knowledge:

> For what is distinctive about this new historical type of democracy is the way *all fields of social and political life* come to be scrutinised, not just by the standard machinery of representative democracy but by a whole host of *non-party, extra-parliamentary* and often *unelected bodies* operating within, underneath and beyond the boundaries of territorial states.[25]

---

23 Keane, *Democracy*, 676.
24 Keane, *Democracy*, 667, 671; see Keane's critical review of Fukuyama's recent book, *Political Order and Political Decay: From the Industrial Revolution to the Globalisation of Democracy*, in *The Age* (Melbourne), 14/2/2015.
25 Keane, *Democracy*, 695 (emphasis in original).

In other words: civil society in the sense of the multiple identities of each citizen increasingly makes its presence felt – at a global level, now reinforced by the ubiquity of social media. This does not amount to romanticising 'the people' but rather to protecting and promoting the dignity of the individual *vis-à-vis* the state and its institutions by means of intermediate organisations. At a level prior to democracy itself, the place of human rights in the process of globalisation becomes apparent.[26]

2.3 Globalisation of Religion?

The above sketch of aspects of globalisation suggests that, whatever its negative characteristics, it may well facilitate and drive the emergence of global civil society. It was also proposed that global civil society by no means implies the continued extension of Western beliefs, values and political structures to the rest of the world. It is, therefore, not to be expected that global civil society will necessarily be 'secular' in the same sense as the purportedly 'neutral' worldview of liberal democratic states.

Examples such as India and Sri Lanka show that this supposed neutrality reaches its limits where societies must contain powerful religious currents in a functional pluralism; as Bellah and his colleagues, commenting on the prospect of a "generalized tolerance", put it: "But tolerance, despite its virtues, is hardly adequate to deal with the conflict and interdependence among different groups in a complex society".[27] In Europe, too, the secularity of liberal democracies is coming under pressure, as the rise of anti-Muslim and pro-Christian nationalism in a number of countries demonstrates.

---

26 Keane, *Democracy*, 709, 734-735.
27 Bellah *et al.*, *Habits of the Heart*, 203.

But if classical civil society in such countries has difficulty coping with the reality of religious pluralism, the global situation is quite different. Here there are no overarching institutions to provide norms or ideological limits for emerging civil society. The ideological mix of Non-Government Organisations (NGOs), religious communities and movements, indigenous ethnic groups, migrants from a variety of cultures, artists, writers and journalists is in constant flux, not to say chaos, symbolised by the Internet, whose information flows are notoriously insecure and difficult to regulate. Even a cursory familiarity with daily events shows that these data streams are strongly influenced by the religions, most dramatically, perhaps, in the recruitment propaganda of Islamic State and the media empires of Christian evangelicals.

The religions' new freedom of movement in virtual space also has repercussions for them in ways that are not sufficiently understood.[28] Global civil society is made up of numerous public spaces, juxtaposed but also overlapping. They penetrate social and political systems regardless of state and territorial boundaries. The religions, too, though cordoned off from one another by their various identity markers, are at the same time mutually porous life worlds. As was mentioned before, they are sub-systems in a larger whole, which – despite their universalist pretentions – they no longer define. To this extent they are all in search of their functions in the overriding system global civil society.

But it is equally true that their interactions help to constitute global civil society. Even those that desperately seek to seal themselves off from 'the world' turn the potential of modernisation to their advantage and thereby participate in globalisation. We may think of American 'televangelists' who make enormous

---

28   Beyer, Peter, *Religions in Global Society* (London and New York: Routledge, 2006); Herbert, David, *Religion and Civil Society: Rethinking Public Religion in the Contemporary World* (Aldershot: Ashgate, 2003).

profits from their own television stations, or Islamists who use the Internet to create a 'virtual *ummah*' in which 'Sheik Google' and 'Imam Facebook' recruit new members, or conservative Buddhists in Thailand who ordain students and other young people as short-term monks and nuns with maximum publicity.

But apart from this the religions have within themselves a considerable potential to criticise mutually exclusive fundamentalisms and counteract the totalitarian tendencies of globalisation. Both the political hegemony aspired to by Islamic State and the overwhelming economic power of multi-national corporations are tendencies which should awaken religious and ethical resistance. The outcome of the global encounter of fundamentalist extremism and ecumenical endeavour is still open.

Over 200 years ago, Immanuel Kant, with remarkable farsightedness, pointed the way to 'perpetual peace' among the peoples.[29] Well aware that his proposal could only be an abstract regulative idea, a categorical imperative of moral reason, Kant nonetheless laid down principles and procedures that would abolish war and institutionalise peace. On the assumption that relations between peoples are analogous to relations between persons, he declared the conclusion of a peace treaty to be an immediate duty. This could only be secured by a truly representative form of government, which for Kant was not democracy – here he shared the scepticism of European thinkers from Plato (*Republic* VIII) to de Tocqueville, who agreed with the American founding fathers that "aristocratic republics had been both more numerous

---

29 Kant, Immanuel, *Zum ewigen Frieden. Ein philosophischer Entwurf* (Stuttgart: Reclam, 1973, orig. 1795); see May, John D'Arcy, "Whose Universality? Which Interdependence? Human Rights, Social Responsibility and Ecological Integrity", Jacques Haers SJ, Norbert Hintersteiner and Georges De Schrijver SJ, eds, *Postcolonial Europe in the Crucible of Cultures: Reckoning with God in a World of Conflicts* (Amsterdam and New York: Rodopi, 2007), 193-211, 195-202.

historically and more enduring than democracies"[30] – but a republican constitution. He envisaged a universal hospitality, a federation of states which would guarantee the rights of all, which we today might call a 'democracy of democracies' (David Held). People should become citizens of the world, for the infringement of their rights in *one* place entails the denial of these rights in *every* place.

Unfortunately, Kant's universalist approach was distorted by the then prevalent racist prejudices, which took for granted that 'yellow', 'red' and 'black' human beings were by nature inferior to 'white' Europeans. Kant nevertheless opened up a vision which only today, in the age of globalisation, comes into its own with the prospect of being realised. The difficulty of his proposal lies in its *a priori* universality. In the end, Kant carries out a transcendental deduction of his own European prejudices, unaware that the universality of his principles could only be negotiated in the exchange of views among widely different religions and cultures.

This observation prompts us to proceed to a survey of the role of the religions – in a wide but fundamental understanding of the term – in the emerging global civil society by investigating a selection of very different civil societies in Asian and Pacific states. We are likely to find that the current categories of Western theology of religions – varieties of exclusivism, inclusivism or pluralism – will be difficult to apply to interreligious relationships and developing theologies in these contexts. The inadequacies of Christian theology in particular will become evident. These questions will be taken up again in Part III. In Part II, we must first turn our attention to the role of the religions in the Asia-Pacific context.

---

30 Bellah *et al.*, *Habits of the Heart*, 254.

PART II

The Religions in Asia-Pacific Societies

Chapter 3: Religious Plurality and Democracy

(Indonesia and Thailand)

In the religious diversity of the Asia-Pacific, just about every religion or type of religion is represented. In the process of globalisation, they are increasingly caught up in an interreligious dynamic which is growing in intensity but is only beginning to unfold. In the midst of this range of religions, Christianity, as a rule (with exceptions such as the Philippines or South Korea), is a small and somewhat intimidated minority.[1] It is little realised that Christianity today is undergoing the most severe persecutions in its entire history, including the first Christian centuries. The International Association for Human Rights estimates that 80 per cent of all antireligious attacks today are directed against Christians. Every year, around 100,000 Christians are killed because of their faith; Christians are discriminated against in 139 countries.[2] In Pakistan, executions because of alleged offences against Islamic piety are not infrequent. In China, North Korea and Vietnam, Christians are subjected to legal restrictions and almost daily persecution. In Indonesia, there are repeated violent conflicts with Christians. The very ancient and numerous Christian populations of Syria and Iraq have been systematically driven out.

---

1   A detailed contemporary portrait of Christianity's situation in Asia may be found in Schmidt-Leukel, Perry, ed., *Buddhist-Christian Relations in Asia* (Sankt Ottilien: EOS Verlag, 2017).
2   See the reports of Patsy McGarry, *The Irish Times,* 23/12/2014, and Paul Vallely, *The Independent,* 27/7/2014. Their thesis, which some commentators find one-sided, was extensively documented by Allen, John, *The Global War on Christians* (New York: Random House, 2013).

Despite this, Christians in Asia and the Pacific Islands are often ecumenically committed and theologically active. The religious traditions that originated in the region (Confucianism, Daoism, Shinto, Hinduism, Buddhism) or have been there for centuries (Christianity, Islam) have been deeply influenced by the geographical and cultural conditions in which they find themselves. The rise of China and India and the consequent challenge to American hegemony have shifted the economic and military balance of power. Island states – especially those which, in deference to China's wishes, refuse to recognise the autonomy of Taiwan – seek investment from China, Australia's main trading partner, but also, in the eyes of some, the greatest threat to its security. I propose to examine two profoundly religious societies which are trying to find their way amidst these tensions: Islamic Indonesia (3.1) and Buddhist Thailand (3.2). We shall then reflect on how their attempts to secure their own versions of democracy shed light on the role of the religions in global civil society (3.3).

3.1 Democracy and Diversity in Indonesia

The transformation of Islam in the modern history of Indonesia illustrates these processes. The indigenous languages and cultures are Malay, but through long-standing trade relationships with India, Hinduism (most visibly on Bali) and Buddhism (especially in Java, to which the monumental temple mountain of Borobudur bears witness) put down deep roots. Islam, too, brought by Arab traders, spread throughout the islands, until Indonesia became the largest Islamic country in the world: 90 per cent of its 250 million inhabitants are nominally Muslim. The smallest of Indonesia's 17,000 islands (the Moluccas, now the province of Maluku) became known in Europe as the 'spice islands', where the medicines and ingredients the Europeans craved could be found.

The country's colonial history was correspondingly colourful and turbulent, until the Dutch secured most of the trade for themselves and founded trading ports such as Batavia, present-day Jakarta.[3]

The early twentieth century saw a contest of identities: there was a new awareness of the Hindu and Buddhist past and a revival of Islam in response to increasing Christian evangelisation (producing the *Sarekat Islam* movement in 1911); the indigenous traditions (*pribumi*) offered resistance to the Dutch, Eurasian, Chinese and Arab influences; and both communists and nationalists grew in numbers, the latter led by the future President Sukarno (1901-1970). Larger and more influential than these, however, was the Islamic popular movement *Muhammadiyah* (founded by Ahmad Dachlan in 1912), which was to play a crucial role in Indonesian politics throughout the twentieth century. These movements survived the Japanese occupation during the Second World War, and, in the subsequent bloody struggles for national self-determination, Sukarno's concept of a secular republic came out on top. It was based on the 'Five Principles' (*Pancasila*):

1. The 'divinity' or 'lordship' of the one universal God (*Ketuhanan Yang Maha Esa*)[4]
2. Universal humanity
3. Nationalism as the pledge of Indonesia's unity
4. Consultative democracy (*shura*)
5. Social justice

---

3   On the colonial period see Owen, N.G., ed., *The Emergence of Modern Southeast Asia: A New History* (Honolulu: University of Hawaii Press, 2005), 53-55; Beck, Herman, *Les Musulmans d'Indonésie* (Turnhout: Éditions Brepols 2003), 11-38.

4   See Sinn, Simone, *Religiöser Pluralismus im Werden. Religionspolitische Kontroversen und theologische Perspektiven von Christen und Muslimen in Indonesien* (Tübingen: Mohr Siebeck, 2014), 134-138, who proposes *all-eine göttliche Herrschaft* or *Gott-Sein des all-einen Gottes* as translations of the first principle, 134-5.

Certain religions (*agama*, namely Islam, Catholicism, Protestantism, Hinduism, later Confucianism, but also indigenous *budaya* or *adat* with their syncretistic mysticism, *abangan*) are recognised as long as they accept these principles. As a result, the religions conform to the state ideology and practise a kind of prescribed ecumenism. Religious pluralism is the normal state of affairs in Indonesia, but it is subject to very specific legal conditions anchored in the constitution. Religious harmony is obligatory, though religious behaviour to a certain – perhaps increasing – degree has *Shari'a* as its norm, especially at local and provincial level.[5]

The situation of Islam was delicate even in earlier times. Arab traders introduced the strict Wahhabi version of the Salafi tradition of jurisprudence from Saudi Arabia in the mid-nineteenth century, which was in tension both with the aristocratic *priyayi* culture deriving from the Hindu-Buddhist past and with the popular mysticism of *abangan*. Sukarno deftly sidestepped these difficulties by retracting an addition to the constitution of the Indonesian Republic, the Jakarta Charter (*Piagam Jakarta*), which would have established *Shari'a* law, the day after independence was declared (18 August 1945). Sukarno's main concern was not Islam but the integrity of the widely scattered and extremely culturally diverse nation. He thereby cleared the way for a 'guided' (i.e. authoritarian) democracy (*Demokrasi Terpimpin*) based on consultation (*shura*) and consensus (*ijma*), for in his eyes Western democracy was un-Indonesian.[6]

---

5   Sinn, *Religiöser Pluralismus*, gives a sensitive analysis of the religious situation, on which I rely in what follows.
6   May, John D'Arcy, "Jakarta and Jayapura: The Dialogue of Religions and 'Papua, Land of Peace'", Carole M. Cusack and Christopher Hartney, eds, *Religion and Retributive Logic: Essays in Honour of Professor Garry W. Trompf* (Leiden and Boston: Brill, 2010), 19-42, 22-31; *id.*, "The Religions and the Powers in West

This created the conditions for Muslims to play a leading but not dominating role in the democratisation of a post-colonial state. The urban and 'modernist' movement *Muhammadiyah* (1912) was soon complemented by the rural and 'traditionalist' *Nahdlatul Ulama* (1926); each had a membership of 30-40 million. Each, therefore, carried considerable weight in the interplay of legal interpretation, religious ethos and political philosophy that characterises Indonesian Islam: ethical and philosophical reflection takes place in the medium of jurisprudence.[7]

Islam in Indonesia has always been plural. To the distinction between the aristocratic *priyayi* and the popular *abangan* cultures, to which that between the officially sanctioned Islam of the nationalists and the 'Javanist' Islam of village dwellers roughly corresponded, was added the tension between secular nationalism and the 'primordial solidarities' (*ikatan primordial*) of the ethnic traditions.[8] Sukarno, on the model of Kemal Atatürk (1881-1938), kept his distance from all varieties of Islam. After his fall in a bloody military putsch in 1965, which General Suharto (1921-2008) used (with the help of *Nahdlatul Ulama*) to slaughter half a million alleged communists, Suharto seized power and became president (1967-1998). His 'New Order' (*Ordre Baru*) tolerated and in the course of time encouraged political activity

---

Papua", Amélé Adamavi-Aho Ekué and Michael Biehl, eds, *Gottesgabe. Vom Geben und Nehmen im Kontext gelebter Religion. Festschrift zum 65. Geburtstag von Theodor Ahrens* (Frankfurt: Lembeck, 2005), 199-213, 201-205.

[7] See Hooker, M.B., *Indonesian Islam: Social Change through Contemporary Fatawa* (Sydney: Allen & Unwin; Honolulu: University of Hawaii Press, 2003); Hefner, Robert, *Civil Islam: Muslims and Democratization in Indonesia* (Princeton: Princeton University Press, 2000).

[8] See Effendy, B., *Islam and the State in Indonesia* (Athens, Ohio: Ohio University Press; Singapore: Institute of Southeast Asian Studies, 2003), and Hefner, *Civil Islam*, 14-16, 50-53, 74-76; Farhadian, C.E., *Christianity, Islam, and Nationalism in Indonesia* (New York and London: Routledge, 2005); Federspiel, H.M., *Islam and Ideology in the Emerging Indonesian State: The Persetuan Islam (PERSIS), 1923 to 1957* (Leiden-Boston-Köln: Brill, 2001).

by Muslims, because he was forced to concede that he could not ignore the Muslim-inspired religiosity of the people if he were to retain power and enrich himself and his family. Religious freedom was guaranteed, but religious life had to conform to the tenets of *Pancasila*. There were sporadic attempts to introduce *Shari'a*, and Islamic boarding schools (*pesantren*) increased in number and influence, but always in tension with popular customs (*adat*). In education, there were conflicts between what was prescribed by the state and attempts to limit state influence.

Under Suharto, nepotism and corruption became so widespread that his fall was inevitable. Islamic parties have never dominated Indonesian politics; they have not even achieved notable majorities. The Islamic popular movements prepared the ground by bringing their social capital to bear in a developing civil society. This opened the way for a remarkable democratic experiment which is still in progress. In many ways, Indonesia today is a religiously and politically pluralist democracy.[9]

Muslim intellectuals have made substantial contributions to this development. Nurcholish Madjid argued for renewal on the basis of *tawhid*, the principle of absolute unity in Islamic monotheism. Abdurrahman Wahid, a leading thinker of the *Nahdlatul Ulama* movement, emphatically advocated pluralism and insisted on the recognition of those who were religiously 'other'. Budhy Munawar-Rachman studied Christian theology of religions and sought ways of justifying pluralism from an Islamic

---

9   Azra, A., "Militant Islamic Movements in Southeast Asia: Sociopolitical and Historical Contexts", *Kultur: The Indonesian Journal for Muslim Cultures* 3/1 (2003), 17-27; *id.*, "The Challenge of Democracy in the Muslim World: Traditional Politics and Democratic Political Culture", K. Helmanita, I. Abubakar, D. Afianty, eds, *Dialogue in the World Disorder: A Response to the Threat of Unilateralism and World Terrorism* (Jakarta: Pusat Bahasa dan Budaya Universitas Islam Negeri Syarif Hidayatulla Jakarta and Konrad Adenauer-Stiftung, 2004), 203-214.

perspective. These and many others prepared the ground for open and many-sided debates about a pluralist Islam.[10]

Even this sketchy account should make clear the main questions in Indonesia's evolving democracy. What exactly is the relationship between Islam and the state? How much influence do the power elites wield in this democracy? How can the environment be protected against the inroads of aggressively expanding commerce, from which the army derives 75 per cent of its funding?[11] To what extent does tourism pose a threat to the country's cultural diversity?

In strictly Islamic Aceh, the practice of religion is overseen by morality police; tolerance of Christians and Shi'ites is in decline. In 2010, a so-called blasphemy law was passed which was actually intended to restrict freedom of religion; in 2005, the Council of Islamic Scholars (*Majelis Ulama Indonesia*, MUI), set up by Suharto in 1975 to strengthen state control, published a *fatwah* forbidding religious pluralism, liberalism and secularism.[12] There was even a law against pornography, whose real purpose was to limit the autonomy of women.

The trial and condemnation of the Christian and ethnic Chinese governor of Jakarta, Basuki Tjahaja Purmama, better known as Ahok, for allegedly blaspheming the *Qur'an* (8 May 2017), shed a harsh light on the religious component in Indonesia's democracy. He was accused of commenting that a verse of the Sura *Al-Maidah* (5:51, "Who is a better judge than Allah for men whose faith is firm? Believers, take neither Jews nor Christians for

---

10 See Sinn, *Religiöser Pluralismus,* Chapter 5, where she also discusses the contributions of Christian theologians; see also Saleh, F., *Modern Trends in Islamic Theological Discourse in Twentieth Century Indonesia: A Critical Survey* (Leiden: Brill, 2001).

11 Leith, Denise, *The Politics of Power: Freeport in Suharto's Indonesia* (Honolulu: University of Hawaii Press, 2003).

12 See Sinn, *Religiöser Pluralismus,* 1-4, 124-126.

your friends"), which, his enemies claimed, prohibited Muslims from being governed by a non-Muslim, was being misused against him by opponents of his re-election. His two year jail sentence was hailed as a victory for radical Islamic conservatives and cast doubt on Indonesia's commitment to a justice system not swayed by popular outrage. On the other hand, the government of President Joko Widodo applied to the courts to disband the hardline group *Hizbut Tahrir Indonesia*, which seeks to establish a global Islamic caliphate.[13]

The media are largely free, various extra-parliamentary movements enliven civil society, and the election which brought Joko Widodo to power marked a surprising change of political direction, given that the military, with its 'double function' (*dwifungsi*) of participating in business and maintaining security, was the *de facto* government. In such a context, civil society has its own structures and functions. We recall that modern Indonesian society took shape according to the norms enshrined in *Pancasila*, which place religious harmony above all else, while everyday life is governed by the ethos of *gotong royong* (cooperation and mutual help), though these principles are not always reflected in the ways the country's institutions function.[14]

On the basis of her extensive interviews with Muslim and Christian intellectuals, Sinn discerns four patterns of discourse which structure debate about pluralism in Indonesia: conflict, diversity, citizenship and proportionality.[15] *Conflict discourse* manifests itself in competing tendencies of 'Christianisation' and 'Islamisation' as they affect matters such as interfaith marriage or the building of churches and mosques. Both communities,

---

13   *The Sydney Morning Herald*, 10/5/2017.
14   Sinn, *Religiöser Pluralismus*, 338-339.
15   Sinn, *Religiöser Pluralismus*, 340-358.

Christian and Muslim, contain liberal and conservative elements, but foreign influence is often made responsible for antagonisms within Indonesia. This is a problem with regard to the overarching imperatives of political stability and religious harmony, and for these the religions themselves are ultimately responsible, the more so since religion is at the very heart of Indonesian identity. Religious pluralism, however, is seen in a *multi*religious rather than an *inter*religious light: the different traditions are more interested in maintaining their boundaries rather than overcoming them by engaging in dialogue.[16]

Diversity discourse has as its context the national motto *Bhinneka tungal ika* (different yet one). It corresponds to the deeply held conviction that Indonesia without diversity is inconceivable. Sinn's interviewees give many examples of interreligious harmony at village and family level.[17] Harmony was anchored in the life of Indonesian society long before the state emerged, but more recently there is evidence of "fanaticism and fundamentalism which values one's own religion higher than others".[18] This is seen as something new and disturbing, more characteristic of Arab countries or Malaysia than Indonesia. Nevertheless, the basic conviction that difference is not negative still pervades discourse about diversity, though there is a need to establish the theological legitimacy of religious diversity among Islamic scholars.[19]

If the themes of conflict and diversity both occur in the framework of a shared concept of reciprocity, *citizenship discourse* strives to assert the basic rights of citizens in the face of discrimination and injustice. The constitution upholds religious freedom, but this is not always apparent in the treatment of

---

16 See Sinn, *Religiöser Pluralismus*, 345-346.
17 Sinn, *Religiöser Pluralismus*, 346-347.
18 Sinn, *Religiöser Pluralismus*, 348.
19 Sinn, *Religiöser Pluralismus*, 348-349.

minorities such as the *Ahmadiyah* movement, the Baha'i or the Jehovah's Witnesses. In practice, the state institutions are often actively involved in discrimination or passively permit it. When it comes to making laws at local level, "there is a tug of war between political interests from the side of both political and religious elites".[20]

The MUI issued a *fatwah* in which the *Ahmadiyah* were declared to be *kafir* (infidels), which flies in the face of the high value placed upon diversity, yet during his tenure as president Abdurrahman Wahid (affectionately known as Gus Dur and acknowledged as a "personality of pluralism") reversed the discrimination of minorities under Suharto and saw to it that Confucianism was included among the traditions officially recognised under *Pancasila*.[21] But many are still averse to any notion of a 'liberal' Islam.

Complementing this is what Sinn calls *proportionality discourse*, which takes its cue from the preponderance of the majority religion, Islam, over all others both in the Ministry of Religion and in various bodies right down to village level. As one interviewee summed it up, "in Christian majority regions the Muslims suffer and in Muslim majority regions the Christians suffer".[22] Officials expect to be bribed in order to redress this imbalance. As one lecturer put it, those in the majority think they are already "tolerant enough" and do not want to go so far as to be "just like the West".[23] This way of thinking is governed by the acceptance of an asymmetrical relationship to which by no means all educated people are opposed.

---

20   Sinn, *Religiöser Pluralismus*, 351, quoting one of her interview subjects.
21   Sinn, *Religiöser Pluralismus*, 353.
22   Sinn, *Religiöser Pluralismus*, 356.
23   Sinn, *Religiöser Pluralismus*, 357.

What seems to be lacking is the realisation that "religious pluralism is… a discursive practice in which conflictive and connective ways of dealing with sameness and difference are constantly being worked out". This seems to indicate that "there is great instability and insecurity, economically, politically and psychologically, among the Indonesian population". Religion is inseparable from power, but by the same token it is a public phenomenon, not relegated to the private sphere as it is in the rhetoric of secularity. *Pancasila* turns out to be a middle way between the "dead ends of an Islamic state and a secularist state". If the religions' teachings mark out the differences between them, socioculturally people live according to what binds them together.[24] Indonesia's pluralism is a dialectical pluralism in which many factors are in tension on many levels. Perhaps it is this that makes it particularly relevant to the complex pluralism of global civil society.

3.2 Buddhism and Democracy in Thailand

Thailand gives every appearance of being the exemplar of a Buddhist nation rather than a religiously diverse one. Except for the rebellious Muslim south, Theravada Buddhism permeates all areas and all institutions right up to the king, who is revered as a traditional *devaraja*, 'divine ruler', or even as a *bodhisattva*, an 'enlightenment being' on his way to Buddhahood. But underneath this harmonious surface, there are complicated relationships between Buddhism and popular religion as there are between Buddhism, Christianity and Islam, and the society is riven by struggles between the urban middle class and rural peasants.[25]

---

24 Sinn, *Religiöser Pluralismus*, 362-364.
25 Marshall, Andrew, *Thailand: A Kingdom in Crisis* (London: Zed Books, 2014).

Throughout Thailand (formerly Siam), Laos, Cambodia and Myanmar (formerly Burma), one finds remnants of the great Khmer empire, from the Buddhist ruins in the style of Hindu temples at Phimai in northeast Thailand to the magnificent remains of Angkor Wat in Cambodia and Bagan in Myanmar. The Thai kings fought successfully to prevent their territory's being absorbed into the empire. Tai speaking peoples from southern China established kingdoms on the lands of the Mon-Khmer and the Tibetan-Burmese (Lan Na, 1296; Ayudhya, 1350; Sukhothai, 13-15 centuries). These were united under kings Rama IV (Mongkut, 1851-1868), Rama V (Chulalongkorn, 1868-1909) and Rama VI (Wachiwarut, 1910-1925), enlightened modernisers who protected their country from the threat of colonialism. The kingdom defended itself successfully from the incursions of Britain and France – which elsewhere in the region set themselves up as colonial masters – more by skilful diplomacy than by war. But Rama VII (Prajadhipok) was deposed in 1932, and the constitutional monarchy that followed was powerless to prevent the rise of the dictators Phibul and Sarit.[26] Nevertheless, the recently deceased King Bhumibol Adulyadej (Rama IX, 1927-2016), who acceded to the throne after the mysterious death of his elder brother Ananda in 1946, was revered as a *bodhisattva*, and criticism of the royal house (*lèse majesté*) is a capital offence.

The mythologising of the Thai monarchy reached absurd levels as the king's final illness took hold in 2009, when it was illegal even to mention the fact that he was close to death. Bhumibol intervened in politics to call the military to account after the brutal suppression of popular protests in 1973 and 1992, but he apparently did nothing to prevent the royalist faction from

---

26 Stowe, Judith A., *Siam Becomes Thailand: A Story of Intrigue* (Honolulu: University of Hawaii Press, 1991).

undermining the popular prime minister Thaksin Shinawatra in 2006. It remains to be seen how his successor, his only son crown prince Vajiralongkorn, will fill the role of king.

China has left its mark on Thailand, but the Japanese failed to conquer it during the Second World War. On closer inspection, Thailand is a patchwork quilt of indigenous and Chinese cultures, exemplified in the Tai-speaking mountain tribes. These, and not the Buddhist *sangha*, shape the culture of the rural population. While the villagers follow their customs and celebrate their life-affirming festivals, the monks remain at a distance; their role is to offer consolation at times of suffering and bereavement. The Buddhist Order remains apolitical but is determined to preserve its autonomy, and through its temple schools and the Ministry of Religion it is everywhere present.[27] It is perhaps not too great an oversimplification to say that modern Thai society rests on three pillars: monarchy, monkhood and military.

This structure is not as stable as the traditional equilibrium between king, *sangha* and people, which formed the basis of historical Buddhist societies such as Sri Lanka.[28] It provided for alliances of monks and people against unjust monarchs, though more often it allowed collusion between king and *sangha* at the expense of the people. Its main danger was the ideologising of religion and the loss of its liberative potential. Buddhism ended up legitimising political power, no matter how corrupt and authoritarian.

After a series of wise and strong kings, since the establishment of constitutional monarchy in 1932, democracy has never really

---

27   See Stowe, *Siam Becomes Thailand*; May, John D'Arcy, *Transcendence and Violence: The Encounter of Buddhist, Christian and Primal Traditions* (London & New York: Continuum, 2003), Chapter 4; Tambiah, S.J., *World Conqueror and World Renouncer: A Study of Buddhism and Polity in Thailand against a Historical Background* (Cambridge: Cambridge University Press, 1976).

28   Pye, Michael, *The Buddha* (London: Duckworth, 1979), 57.

been on a firm footing in Thailand. Again and again, military putsches have taken place with the not entirely implausible justification that politicians have been too much concerned with their own enrichment and have paid scant attention to the stark disparity between city and countryside, rich and poor. With the ailing king withdrawing more and more from public life, these tensions exploded into violent clashes between 'red shirts' (poor peasants) and 'yellow shirts' (urban monarchists). The king seems to have favoured the royalists; the *sangha* was ineffectual and slow to react. An important opportunity to redefine Buddhism on the global public stage – as happened briefly in Myanmar with the 'saffron revolution', the popular revolt led by monks in 2007 – has been lost.

But long before these conflicts developed, the blueprint for progressive and pluralist Buddhism in Thailand was sketched by Buddhadasa Bhikkhu. He was a traditional monk who underwent the usual training in Pali language and the canonical texts in Bangkok but became disillusioned with the conservative Buddhist establishment. He saw more serious problems than the correct performance of courtly ceremonies, and he began to read the Buddhist sources for himself. He criticised the kind of Buddhism that ignored the needs of the people and legitimised the existing social order. He withdrew to the forests of southern Thailand and founded a hermitage called *Suan Mokh*, 'Garden of Liberation', where he formulated a 'dhammic socialism' with the aim of adapting socialism to Asian conditions.[29]

His ideas did not come from the European Enlightenment – his easily misunderstood concept of 'dictatorial democracy' is evidence of that – but he was an original thinker. He influenced

---

29 Buddhadasa Bhikkhu, *Dhammic Socialism*, ed. Donald Swearer (Bangkok: Thai Inter-Religious Commission for Development, 1986).

a whole generation of intellectuals and activists such as the lay Buddhist social critic Sulak Sivaraksa, the so-called 'development monks' in poorer areas, and the international movement of 'socially engaged Buddhism'.[30] He had no difficulty in adopting elements of other Buddhist traditions such as Zen, and he engaged in theological dialogue with Christians and Muslims. For him, 'God' and *dhamma* were in principle the same.

His interpretation of Buddhism was pragmatic. His was a Buddhism for the here and now, not for a scarcely conceivable Beyond unattainable for ordinary mortals. He was, therefore, socially committed and critical; the transcendent 'language of the *dhamma*' was the inner dimension of the 'language of the world' and was thus immanent in politics, society and environment. He inspired a generation of Buddhist social critics such as Sulak, whose 'radical conservatism'[31] incessantly criticises the undermining of democracy by politicians and generals. For his pains he has been repeatedly persecuted and arrested on trumped up charges of *lèse majesté*.[32] Perhaps the best distillation of his thinking is his *Seeds of Peace*, in which he outlines an approach to economic justice and non-violent activism inspired by Buddhist principles.[33] We shall

---

30   Queen, Christopher S., and Sallie B. King, eds, *Engaged Buddhism: Buddhist Liberation Movements in Asia* (Albany, NY: State University of New York Press, 1996), Chapter 5.

31   Sivaraksa, Sulak, ed., *Radical Conservatism: Buddhism in the Contemporary World. Articles in Honour of Bhikkhu Buddhadasa's 84th Birthday Anniversary* (Bangkok: Thai Inter-Religious Commission for Development, International Network of Engaged Buddhists, 1990). The range of articles in this *Festschrift* by authors from East and West shows the depth and extent of Buddhadasa's influence.

32   Sivaraksa, Sulak, *Siamese Resurgence: A Thai Buddhist Voice on Asia and a World of Change* (Bangkok: Asian Cultural Forum on Development, 1985), where a selection of his essays on development, ecology and education is accompanied by a documentation of his various trials and clashes with authorities.

33   Sivaraksa, Sulak, *Seeds of Peace: A Buddhist Vision for Renewing Society* (Berkeley: Paralax Press, 1992). The *Festschrift* presented to Sulak on his 70th birthday gives an impression of the range of his friendships and the scope of his

return to this strand of critical thinking in Chapter 6 on economic ethics.

In conclusion, however, it must be noted that there are also movements in Thai Buddhism, such as *Wat Thammakay* and *Santi Asok*, which propagate Buddhist ethics as bourgeois morality. Not unlike the role of Islamic jurisprudence in Indonesia, in Thailand, Buddhist doctrine is appropriated as the medium of political debate.[34] The upwardly striving lower and upper middle classes in the cities with their rational cast of mind are impatient under the yoke of the monkish establishment. Buddhadasa rationalised the supernatural and placed it squarely on the ground of social reality, but his intentions were ethical, not political. Phra Potirak, too, broke with the monastic establishment and his puritanical movement *Santi Asok* indirectly criticised political corruption and the misuse of power by the military, but like Buddhadasa he shied away from participating in politics. For social critics like Sulak Sivaraksa and Prawase Wasi, such movements are symptoms, not the sickness itself. Although they remind one of Evangelical or Pentecostal fundamentalists, they see in Buddhism an antidote to the materialism and liberalism of a rapidly developing society.

For outsiders, it is not easy to discern the public effectiveness of such movements: the familiar labels 'liberal', 'progressive', 'traditional' or 'conservative' do not capture the significance of these personalities and their initiatives, for they derive from the deep connection between the spiritual and the worldly roles of the *chakravartin*, 'he who turns the wheel (of spiritual or earthly affairs)'. Traditionally, this was manifested in the person of the

---

influence, Chappell, David W., ed., *Socially Engaged Spirituality: Essays in Honor of Sulak Sivaraksa on His 70th Birthday* (Bangkok: Sathirakoses-Nagapradipa Foundation, 2003).

34   Jackson, Peter A., *Buddhism, Legitimation, and Conflict: The Political Functions of Urban Thai Buddhism* (Singapore: Institute of Southeast Asian Studies, 1989), 7, 55.

devaraja or 'divine king', but today the ideal must be transposed to pluralist democratic societies such that Buddhist spirituality, philosophy and ethics can influence policymaking.[35] The fusion of Buddhism and monarchy, and the sophisticated social criticism of contemporary Buddhist thinkers, can only be understood against this background.[36]

3.3 The Deeper Dimensions of Democratic Pluralism

Throughout Southeast Asia, there is a growing tendency for autocratic rulers to manipulate the democratic process in order to entrench themselves in power, brushing aside criticism until they are beyond the reach of would-be rivals. In such a context, Indonesia and Thailand appear as vigorous democracies, opening themselves – with occasional lapses into authoritarianism – to political and religious pluralism. Moreover, in the cases of both Islamic Indonesia and Buddhist Thailand this is happening on the basis of traditional religious culture. These developments – the turn to democracy in Indonesia, the slow transformation of Buddhism as the state religion in Thailand – hint at the role the religions could play in a global pluralist public sphere which is by no means simply 'secular'.

In both cases, as we shall see, the national religions face ethical challenges – human rights, especially those of minorities; economic justice; ecological responsibility; gender equality – which are central in the global context. The credibility and the ethical principles of both traditions, Islam and Buddhism, are

---

35 Tambiah, *World Conqueror and World Renouncer*; id., *Buddhism and the Spirit Cults in North-east Thailand* (Cambridge: Cambridge University Press, 1970), 74; May, *Transcendence and Violence*, 87-92.

36 Harris, Ian, ed., *Buddhism and Politics in Twentieth-Century Asia* (London and New York: Pinter, 1999); Haynes, Jeff, *Religion in Third World Politics* (Buckingham and Philadelphia: Open University Press, 1993).

thus put to the test. The response of both countries to the refugee problem, as we shall see in Chapter 7, has international relevance. In this way, religious impulses are being gradually fed into the constantly developing consensus of global civil society.

Implicit in these observations are fundamental questions to which we must return. One concerns the relationship between religion and morality: can moral principles and norms be in any way derived from religious teachings? In a more general sense, do political ethics and the structuring of civil society depend on particular worldviews? In the Christian West, the answer to this question has been affirmative, not least in the social doctrine of the Catholic Church, but also in calls for a return to 'Christendom' in Europe.

The most problematic version of this assumption is perhaps the 'political theology' of the Catholic jurist and political scientist Carl Schmitt, who, as a result of the traumatic experiences of the Weimar Republic in pre-war Germany, saw democracy itself in danger.[37] On 1 May 1933, at the instigation of Heidegger, he joined the Nazi party and remained a member till 1945, protected by Goering, so it is not surprising that his seminal treatise, *Political Theology: Four Chapters on the Concept of Sovereignty*, was not translated into English for 63 years.[38]

Here, I shall refer to a contemporary re-conceptualising of Schmitt's rather enigmatic reasoning by Paul Kahn.[39] For Kahn, the idea that the religious is simply evaporating from Western

---

37 May, John D'Arcy, "Political Theology Revisited", in O'Grady, John; Cathy Higgins; Jude Lal Fernando, eds, *Mining Truths: Festschrift in Honour of Geraldine Smyth OP – Ecumenical Theologian and Peacebuilder* (St. Ottilien: EOS Verlag, 2015), 537-554, 541-549. In what follows I reproduce parts of this essay.

38 Schmitt, Carl, *Political Theology: Four Chapters on the Concept of Sovereignty* (Chicago and London: University of Chicago Press, 1985), translated by George Schwab from the revised German edition of 1934.

39 Kahn, Paul W., *Political Theology: Four New Chapters on the Concept of Sovereignty* (New York: Columbia University Press, 2011).

civilisation, leaving a residue of the purely secular, is wrong-headed and ignores the origins of European institutions in Christian forebears. For Schmitt, there is something theological about the very notion of the nation-state and the concept of popular sovereignty on which it is based. This connotes an originating act of will, what he calls the decision *aus dem Nichts* ('out of nothing'), and the imperative of sacrifice.[40]

In at least some liberal theory, the state's prerogative of violence is not accounted for, and the possibility of war is not present. We realise that the sovereignty of the nation-state is the stumbling block of all well-meaning schemes to establish international structures and enforce international law. If the sovereign is the people, who speaks for them?[41] If there is continuity between the modern nation-state and the theological tradition, and if this no longer consists in the church's dominance of politics, what forms does it take and how are we to estimate its influence? The church may have been defeated, but the secular never won: the search for meaning continually disturbs the efficiencies of law and commerce.[42] "To confront Schmitt is, accordingly, to confront the most fundamental issue in theorizing the character and meaning of the modern state", namely "that the state creates and maintains its own sacred space and history".[43]

Rather than ascribing the origin of the state to the social contract, Schmitt contends that it is popular sovereignty that enables the social contract in the first place. Claims of national political identity trump first principles; indeed, reason and the people themselves are ritualised and sacralised in order to legitimate

---

40   Kahn, *Four New Chapters*, 17; see 62-64.
41   Kahn, *Four New Chapters*, 10.
42   Kahn, *Four New Chapters*, 26.
43   Kahn, *Four New Chapters*, 18, 19.

sacrifice, the wellspring of revolution and war alike.[44] Far from religion's having been made private, as liberal theory assumes, the supposedly secular state draws deeply on the experience of faith: "The political formation of the experience of the sacred is the subject of political theology".[45]

Crucial to Schmitt's theory – and missing from most modern accounts of liberalism – is what he calls 'the exception': the unforeseen crisis that threatens to tear asunder the whole structure of laws and norms and with it the polity itself. The opening sentence of Schmitt's first chapter on sovereignty, "Sovereign is he who decides on the exception", amounts to a "dialectical negation of liberal political theory".[46] The exception is by definition not the norm, and in dealing with the exception one is not simply applying the norm but making a decision beyond its scope. The function of the norm is to allow us to identify the exception and contextualise the act of sovereign will: "no exception, no sovereignty".[47] The state must continually will itself into being.

Schmitt's claim that every political order corresponds to a metaphysical world view may be reductionist, but his further claim is worthy of consideration: neither norms nor extraneous causes are the origin of law; rather, the judicial decision itself is a statement of the law rather than the mere application of an already existing principle.[48] He captures the interplay between social practices and ideas: "A practice... is not the end of discourse but is itself a form of discourse. A practice always expresses a symbolic content; it stands to ideas in the same way that a proposition does".[49]

---

44   Kahn, *Four New Chapters*, 21.
45   Kahn, *Four New Chapters*, 23, 24.
46   Kahn, *Four New Chapters*, 31.
47   Kahn, *Four New Chapters*, 46.
48   See Kahn, *Four New Chapters*, 95, 98-99, 115.
49   Kahn, *Four New Chapters*, 99, see 93.

Thought, action and faith are always in a kind of interplay.⁵⁰

Schmitt failed to account for the diversity, contingency and *bricolage* that characterise pluralism, but his scrutiny of the presuppositions of democracy sounds a warning: confronted by an existential threat, such as the rise of fascism, the proliferation of terrorism or the so-called refugee crisis, popular sovereignty has recourse to the call to sacrifice, not to legal obligations arising from the social contract. But "[l]iberal theory… fails even to see the problem" that this poses. "A politics that is complete in itself, that wants only to realize its own truth, touches on the sacred",⁵¹ the implication being that when its identity and its very existence are threatened, it defends this truth to the last drop of blood as a sacred duty. With this we are ominously close to the rationales of such organisations as the IRA or Islamic State.

Schmitt himself, Kahn concludes, overwhelmed by circumstances in the Weimar chaos, chose authenticity over justice. His powerful leading idea, that sacrifice is "the appearance of the sacred as a historical phenomenon", admonishes us that the call to decision, to respond to the exception rather than conform to the norm, can come to anyone at any time. To embrace the exception is to realise in our own lives "an ultimate meaning".⁵² Schmitt's theories led him to the dead end of acquiescing in fascism, but they remind us that radical questioning of the very idea of democracy can emerge within the Western tradition.

Similar questions exercise Islamic thinkers, such as the Tunisian Rachid Ghannouchi.⁵³ He too asks whether liberal democracy necessarily entails secularism, or whether the

---

50   See Kahn, *Four Chapters*, 100.
51   Kahn, *Four New Chapters*, 121-122.
52   Kahn, *Four New Chapters*, 155, 158, see 153.
53   See Glancy, Brian, *Liberalism Without Secularism? Rachid Ghannouchi and the Theory and Politics of Islamic Democracy* (Dublin: Columba Press, 2007).

inalienable rights of the individual are more important than the particular worldviews that legitimise them.[54] The challenge of Islamism is that it "seek[s] to integrate religious norms and values within the political system", thereby creating "an authentic and indigenous alternative to secularism".[55] Islamism is not necessarily fundamentalist, opposed to humanism and reason; it is "located in the space that is freed through the deconstruction of the relationship between the West and modernity".[56]

The thesis is that what was traditionally called 'just Islamic rule' (*hakimiyyah*), rather than liberalism, would be the basis of Islamic democracy as an alternative to Westernisation.[57] It was aggressive secularism, after all, not Islamism, that led to a series of dictatorships in the Arab world. The sort of civil society that existed in Muslim countries, very different from that in the West, was not allowed to form the basis of a pluralist democracy,[58] a pressure which Indonesian civil society successfully resisted, as we have seen. The processes now unfolding in various Muslim countries touch on the unresolved question of the relation between revelation and reason in Islam and the central issue of sovereignty. Abdolkarim Soroush "sees the use of a kind of public or collective reason as fundamental to the project of Islamic renewal".[59]

Equally important are the toleration of diversity and the treatment of apostasy as presuppositions of religious pluralism in societies based on Islamic values. Given that there is a "growing public sphere in the Islamic world", it may not be too much to

---

54   Glancy, *Liberalism*, 9-10, citing Katerina Dalacoura, *Islam, Liberalism and Human Rights*.
55   Glancy, *Liberalism*, 13.
56   Glancy, *Liberalism*, 15, citing Ismail, *Rethinking Islamist Politics*.
57   Glancy, *Liberalism*, 17, 20.
58   Glancy, *Liberalism*, 31-32.
59   Glancy, *Liberalism*, 26, citing Soroush, *Reason, Freedom and Democracy in Islam*; see 28.

expect that "civic virtue is derived from something other than .. secular, Enlightenment foundations ... and it is what allows the non-secular state to transcend itself and make the claim to liberalism".[60] Glancy concludes that "it is arguable that religious reasons provide the deepest and most secure foundation for the liberal commitment to equality, freedom, and the human being as a value in him- or herself".[61] Whether this proposal is really feasible is yet to be demonstrated as Islamic societies struggle to reconcile diversity with consensus and find their place in the emerging global order. But, at the very least, it provides a point of orientation as we go on to examine other civil societies inspired by the religions of the Asia-Pacific.

---

60   Glancy, *Liberalism*, 52; see
61   Glancy, *Liberalism*, 47.

Chapter 4: Buddhism, Peace and Violence

(Sri Lanka and Japan)

Throughout Southeast Asia, Buddhism, Christianity and Islam, albeit in very different ways, are strongly interwoven with politics,[1] just as Christianity has decisively influenced the political development of Pacific Island states. Traditionally, Buddhism has accommodated itself to virtually every type of government, as long as the *sangha* is left in peace to pursue its otherworldly ideals. But monks have led many a revolt against intolerable circumstances, as has happened in recent memory in Myanmar and Thailand and in the past in Sri Lanka and Japan, for as a rule the monks are close to the people.

In Islam, almost the opposite is the case: the Islamic ideal is the Islamic state, and where Muslims have come to terms with existing cultures and structures more radical influences are at work which would remodel society according to *Shari'a* law. Catholicism in the Philippines and Protestantism in South Korea fall between these extremes: in both cases, Christians have strongly opposed dictatorial regimes and they are reconciled to the pluralism of democratic societies. Islam, too, although infiltrated by Salafi fundamentalists in places like the southern Philippines, southern Thailand, Malaysia and Indonesia, flourishes in these societies and gives an example to Muslims in very different contexts, from the Middle East to the West.

Buddhism, however, is confronted by problems that it is ill-equipped to solve, especially where social or international

---

1   Harris, Ian, ed., *Buddhism and Politics in Twentieth-Century Asia* (London and New York: Pinter, 1999).

conflicts become violent. We are going to look more closely at two such cases: the entanglement of the *sangha* in a brutal civil war in Sri Lanka (4.1) and the legitimising of Japanese militarism by Buddhist traditions (4.2). Each of these episodes raises ethical and doctrinal questions every bit as fundamental as those posed to European Christianity by the rise of Nazism and the Holocaust. In conclusion, we will examine the more general issue of the motivation or mitigation of violence by religions as it relates to their role in global civil society (4.3). Later, we shall have to address the appalling situation in Myanmar, where a purportedly Buddhist population is egged on by the army, fanatical monks and a militarily controlled government to treat Muslim Rohingya and other ethnic minorities with genocidal cruelty.

4.1 The Radicalisation of Buddhism in Sri Lanka

The island of Lanka nestles against the south-eastern coast of the Indian subcontinent (present-day Tamil Nadu), an area populated by Dravidian Tamils from time immemorial. Here Hinduism is characterised by elaborate temples and passionate devotion (*bhakti*). According to the *Ramayana*, an epic beloved in the whole of south Asia, Sita, the spouse of Prince Rama, is stolen by Ravana, the evil king of Lanka, whence she is liberated with the help of the monkey king Hanuman. Legendary stories of this type, as we shall see, play a very important role in Asian societies, where to this day they influence the mentality of the people and the elites.

The Sri Lankan national epic narrates how Mahinda, the son of the Buddhist emperor Asoka, brought Buddhism to Lanka with a cutting from the Tree of Enlightenment (*Bodhi*), under which the ascetic Gautama became the Buddha ('Enlightened One'). From this branch, the sacred tree in the temple compound of

Anuradhapura, a former capital of Lanka, is said to have grown. In the *Mahavamsa*, the 'Great Chronicle' of the island of Lanka (*Lankadipa*), another 'evil king', Duttagamini ('evil Dutta'), plays a central role. The chronicle tells us how the Buddha is supposed to have visited the island in a miraculous way. Duttagamini, like Asoka before him, is converted and becomes a pious Buddhist ruler. The Tamil Elara, although he is portrayed as the enemy who tries to force Hinduism upon the people, is characterised as an honourable man, while his Buddhist opponent is described as wicked. Monks assure Duttagamini that the killing of Hindu enemies in battle is not a crime, for they are sub-human. This very passage was used in recent times to justify atrocities against Tamils in Sri Lanka's civil war. Sri Lanka attains mythical significance as the predestined home of authentic Buddhism.

The Palk Strait, which separates Sri Lanka from India, is neither wide nor deep, which explains why Tamils have lived on the island of Lanka from time immemorial. Theravada Buddhism, whose purity is the pride of the Singhalese, has been strongly influenced by Hinduism and its iconography displays Mahayanist elements. The Singhalese regard themselves as Aryans (stemming from north India, the Buddha's home country) and thus as the 'original' Buddhists, the most authentic in Asia. The dark-skinned Tamils of south India, on the other hand, are seen as traditional enemies who repeatedly tried to conquer the island. Here, and not in the presence of Tamil workers on the tea plantations, who were introduced much later by the British colonial masters, lie the roots of the deplorable civil war which broke out after independence in 1948 and raged until recently.

Ceylon, as it was called in colonial times, in contrast to virtually untouched Thailand, experienced three waves of colonisation: first by the (Catholic) Portuguese, then by the (Calvinist) Dutch, and finally by the (Anglican and Methodist) British. Each period of foreign rule left deep traces, affecting the family traditions and religious convictions of the population. The Buddhists, who are almost exclusively Singhalese, are the dominant majority with about 69 per cent, but the Muslims (7.5 per cent), descended from Arab traders, and the Christians of different denominations (7.5 per cent) are significant minorities.

The largely Hindu Tamils (17 per cent), who called whole areas in the north and east their own, remained a foreign body in this religiously diverse society. Even so, relations between these sectors of the population would not have been so conflicted if the Singhalese, after independence in 1948, had not stubbornly attempted to carry out a policy of exclusive Singhalese-Buddhist dominance, manifested above all since 1956 in the takeover of the elite English-speaking schools established by the Christians and the language policy of 'Sinhala alone'. These efforts were inspired by Buddhist reformers such as Anagarika Dharmapala (1864-1933), who set out to reinstate the purity of Singhalese Buddhism, made the Buddhist holy place Bodh Gaya in north India accessible to the faithful and approved of an uprising against Muslims in 1915.

These policies sowed the seed of ethnically and religiously determined nationalism, which bore fruit in a bloody civil war. The aggressive self-assertion of the Singhalese prompted resistance by the Tamils, peaceful at first, who also sought to preserve their autonomy. In 1971, there followed an armed revolt of the Buddhist-inspired People's Liberation Front (*Janata Vimukthi Peramuna*, JVP) in response to economic decline and unemployment among Singhalese. After the bloody repression of student unrest in 1983, the organisation known as the Tamil Tigers emerged as a violent liberation movement. This in turn called forth the Buddhist movement *Sinhala Veera Vidhana* (SVV), also violent and supported by nationalistic militant monks. The defence of the unitary Buddhist state was equated with the defence of the *dhamma* itself.

This identification of being Singhalese with being Buddhist seriously compromised the *sangha*, because it awakened to new life the centuries old justification of violence against Indian enemies in the *Mahavamsa*. The conflict devastated the island for decades until the last remnants of the Tamil Tigers were brutally exterminated in 2009, preparing the way for a government that was democratic in appearance only. The brutal and corrupt President Rajapaksa, however, was surprisingly defeated in the election of 2014, giving some hope of genuine reconciliation and pacification. Mainly Tamil refugees, however, are still trying escape persecution by the Singhalese, attempting to reach Australia or New Zealand in dilapidated fishing boats. Whereas New Zealand has offered at least some of them asylum, Australia forcibly sends them back or interns them before they have even reached its borders, as we shall see in Chapter 7.

Sri Lanka has a long tradition of interreligious dialogues, initiatives and radical movements. These have been both Christian (like the *Tulana* dialogue centre founded by the Jesuit Aloysius Pieris or Tissa Balasuriya's Centre for Society and Religion) and Buddhist in inspiration (for example, the rural development movement *Sarvodaya Shramadana* led by the Buddhist layman A. T. Ariaratne). In the face of surging ethnic-religious nationalism, understandably, they have been unable to turn the tide, but their longer term significance should not be underestimated.

In the struggle against the Tamils, Buddhism has been radicalised and even militarised to the point where a party composed of monks, the Sri Lanka Heritage Party (JHU), has taken a hard line and supported the military, though the excesses of the

Rajapaksa regime led to their leaving the governing coalition. The plural interreligious relations which, despite all this, continued to characterise the religious atmosphere were seriously compromised.[2] Already in colonial times there were acrimonious public debates between representatives of Buddhism and Christianity,[3] but in the course of time a more ecumenical spirit prevailed, and remarkable centres of dialogue appeared, such as Aloysius Pieris's *Tulana*, already mentioned, and the Ecumenical Centre for Study and Dialogue founded by the Methodist pioneer of dialogue Lynn A. de Silva, while Tissa Balasuriya OMI (1924-2013) devoted himself to the study of social questions in cooperation with Buddhists and Muslims (and for his pains was excommunicated by John Paul II's Vatican in 1997, mainly because of alleged 'relativism' in his book *Mary and Human Liberation*).

When I visited Sri Lanka in 1979, I was deeply impressed by these and other centres, institutes and movements, but I wondered what would happen when their charismatic founders had passed on.[4] It is nothing less than tragic that these initiatives have been swamped by Buddhist nationalism.[5] The tragedy is only deepened by the fact that Buddhism, in the light of its fatal identification

---

2   Hettiarachchi, Shanthikumar, *Faithing the Native Soil: Dilemmas and Aspirations of Post-Colonial Buddhists and Christians in Sri Lanka* (Colombo: Centre for Society and Religion, 2012), which is to be treated with caution, as it turns out to be biased towards the Tamils.

3   Harris, Elizabeth J., *Theravāda Buddhism and the British Encounter: Religious, Missionary and Colonial Experience in Nineteenth Century Sri Lanka* (London/New York: Routledge, 2006); Harris, Elizabeth J., "Confrontations over Conversions: A Case Study from Sri Lanka", May, John D'Arcy, ed., *Converging Ways? Conversion and Belonging in Buddhism and Christianity* (St Ottilien: EOS Verlag, 2007), 37-54.

4   May, John D'Arcy, "Christian-Buddhist-Marxist Dialogue in Sri Lanka: A Model for Social Change in Asia?", *Journal of Ecumenical Studies* 19 (1982), 719-743.

5   Fernando, L.A. Jude Lal, *Religion, Conflict and Peace in Sri Lanka: The Politics of Interpretation of Nationhoods* (Münster-Wien-Berlin: LIT Verlag, 2013). What follows is based on this thorough and penetrating analysis of the situation.

with racist nationalism, is discredited in the international public sphere as a partner in discussion.

How could it come to this? Fernando shows convincingly that it was not Buddhism alone that led to this sorry state of affairs. It was rather an essentialist conception of religion as a factor in the mythologising of history that led to this unholy alliance between religion and politics.[6] The 'Eelam Tamils', as he calls the peoples of the north and east of the island who have been striving for autonomy for centuries, frustrated by their mere presence the project of constructing a unitary Singhalese-Buddhist nation-state. This project was not originally conceived by the Singhalese but by the British colonial masters, who after popular revolts in 1818 and 1848 – on the doorstep, as it were, of the Indian *Raj* and astride the vitally important trading route between the Indian and Pacific oceans – wanted an island united by the dominant religious ideology.

In throwing off British domination after World War II, the Singhalese adopted the *idea* of nationalism, the successful unitary nation-state, from the British imperialists.[7] This idea became their ideal as they led their country to independence. They learned from the British that this nationalist mission needs a powerful ideology, similar to the then current conception of 'British Israel', a Britain which, like ancient Israel, acted on behalf of God. Indigenous cultures – meaning in this case the foreign religion and language of the Tamils, but also the Muslims and Christians – were to be reduced to a homogeneous unity in order to further this national project. This ideology of unity ignored the fact that there were numerous Buddhist Tamils.

---

6   Fernando, *Religion, Conflict and Peace*, 93-96.
7   Fernando, *Religion, Conflict and Peace*, 96-107.

An important factor in British thinking, as it was to be later in American security policy, was the deep water harbour of Trincomalee on the east coast, which was not allowed to be inside or near an area controlled by Tamils. When the EU, with Indian support, approved a peace plan initiated by Norway in 2002, the US, with the consent of the United Kingdom, declared the Tamil Tigers to be a terrorist organisation, which made further negotiations impossible. It was in the interest of the Anglo-Saxon powers to 'solve' the Tamil question, just as it had been in the colonial politics of the nineteenth century.

Fernando characterises the Singhalese war against the Tamils as a war against democracy and the brutal 'victory' of 2009 as the defeat of democracy, for "the attacks against the Muslims by the Sinhala Buddhist nationalist groups have increased in an unprecedented manner after the Sri Lankan government's military victory over the LTTE".[8] He sees in this conflict not so much a clash of cultures as a contradiction in the interpretation of nationalism based on essentialist conceptions of religion, ethnicity and nationhood.[9] Space is thus created for ideas such as 'pure Singhalese Aryans', uncontaminated by Dravidian Tamils and living in 'liberated' and ethnically 'cleared' areas, while "in the eyes of the Tamil movement for self-determination the 'uncleared areas' are the 'liberated areas'".[10]

This situation is all the more tragic in that all the religions involved have a liberating and peace-building potential which could be more effective than the ultimately futile secular peace initiatives of the Europeans. Both, church and *sangha*, must take responsibility for the hardening of opposition on both sides and

---

8   Fernando, *Religion, Conflict and Peace*, xv.
9   Fernando, *Religion, Conflict and Peace*, 7-10.
10 Fernando, *Religion, Conflict and Peace*, 217; see 217-221.

the worsening of violence, but both also have the potential to transform the unitary ideological nation-state into a pluralistic democracy. Both the conflict and the attempts to resolve it have not just local but global significance. There were numerous local interreligious peace movements which had connections to international efforts in the context of complicated global politics.[11] The Sri Lanka conflict and its provisional outcome exemplify the dynamics of peace work in the context of global civil society. Fernando concludes:

> While strengthening local initiatives for a just-peace, as the local and global issues are interwoven within a network of asymmetrical power relationships among nations, the way out of the conflict lies in addressing the moral consciousness of global civil society in relation to the local situation and thereby formulating a global ethic of just-peace that would support local initiatives. As moral agents, the religions, while accepting their culpability, need to take the responsibility of negotiating a moral imagination of a just-peace with power politics if they are to be credible to the society both on the local and global level.[12]

4.2 Buddhism and Japanese Imperialism

The Japanese, too, look back to a mythical past whose story is told in the chronicles *Kojiki* (712) and *Nihon Shoki* (720). Mud and water detach themselves from the primordial chaos, and in the heavens many goddesses and gods come into being. Two of these,

---

11 Fernando, *Religion, Conflict and Peace*, 229-240.
12 Fernando, *Religion, Conflict and Peace*, 239.

the siblings Izanagi and Izanami, become curious and Izanagi dips his staff into the sea. As he withdraws it, lumps of mud and drops of water fall back into the sea and form the Japanese islands. The pair give birth to the sun goddess Amaterasu Omikami, the moon god Tsukuyomi and their uncontrollable brother Susano-o, who devastates the earth with wind and storm. The first Japanese emperor, Jimmu, is descended from Ninigi, Amaterasu's son. The land itself and the imperial family are thus of divine origin, which forms the basis of the Japanese national religion, Shinto.

The ancient documents are composed in Chinese script and testify to the influence of Chinese culture on Japanese civilisation. Buddhism, too, came to Japan via Korea from China from the sixth century on, and together with Confucianism was a decisive factor in the unification of Japan by means of the constitution of Prince Shotoku Taishi (604). The underlying basis of Japanese religiosity, however, remained the deep relationship to the land itself, which by virtue of this divine origin was regarded as sacred, a relationship embodied in the person of the emperor (*tenno*). The determining factor in Japanese religion to this day is thus simply 'Japaneseness' (*nihonjinron*). It finds expression in the rites of Shinto, which in their closeness to nature symbolise reverence for the *kami* (the supernatural powers inherent in natural phenomena, above all in the *tenno* himself) and carry out ritual purification by water, salt and fire.[13]

Here lie the causes of a certain bifurcation between popular and courtly Buddhism. The introduction of a sinicised Buddhism was pioneered by Saicho (Dengyo Daishi, 767-822) and Kukai (Kobo Daishi, 774-835). Both obtained permission to study in China, Saicho at Mount Tien-tai in 804. In the same year, Kukai

---

13   See Beasley, W.G., *The Japanese Experience: A Short History of Japan* (London: Phoenix Press, 2000), Chapter 1; May, *Transcendence and Violence*, Chapter 3.

visited the Tang capital Chang-an. Saicho spent his whole life working towards the acceptance of ordination according to the Tien-tai (Jap. Tendai) Mahayana rite on the temple mountain of Hiei near Kyoto, where up to his time only the precepts for lay people were conferred. Had he succeeded, Japanese monks would have been independent of state control, but this was only permitted after his death.

Kukai was beloved among the people because of his active compassion for poor peasants. He tolerated other sects and even Confucian and Daoist teachings. For him the simplest everyday activities were Buddhist practice. The world of the court, however, with its aesthetic and erotic tastes and its constant power struggles, was far removed from such ideals. There, the art of interpreting the religiously venerated *Lotus-Sutra* was the key to political influence among Tendai monks. Eventually, in the latter part of the Heian period, "the general state of Buddhism was one of continued corruption, ambition and cynicism. Increasing rivalry between schools of Buddhism, which by now had their own armies of monk-soldiers, led to bloody fights, burning of temples, and perpetual intrigue".[14] It is thus not surprising that "Buddhism and politics, religion and politics, were not two different phenomena – to do religion was to do politics, and vice versa".[15]

Apart from the cultural exchange with China, Japan was a closed society which sealed itself off from the outside world for two centuries after the arrival of the first traders and missionaries from Europe. To compensate for the forced opening up of Japan by

---

14   Cook, Francis H., "Heian, Kamakura, and Tokugawa Periods in Japan", Charles S. Prebish, ed., *Buddhism: A Modern Perspective* (University Park: Pennsylvania State University Press, 1975), 223-228, 224.

15   McMullin, Neil, "The *Lotus Sutra* and Politics in the Mid-Heian Period", in George J. Tanabe Jr. und Willa Jane Tanabe, eds, *The Lotus Sutra in Japanese Culture* (Honolulu: University of Hawaii Press, 1989), 119-141, 119, 136-137; May, *Transcendence and Violence*, 68-70.

the Americans under the Meiji (1868), the government formally instituted a strengthening of national identity as a defence against the by now inescapable influences from overseas. Shinto suddenly became the religion of Japaneseness in an entirely new sense. Buddhism and Confucianism were now regarded as foreign and had to justify their existence, even to the point of registering their monasteries and temples with the bureaucracy, inasmuch as they had not already been deliberately destroyed.

Buddhism, which should have been above such narrowness on account of its transcendental orientation, made haste to appear as 'national' as possible. Zen, in particular, which cultivated deep insight into the emptiness of all human desiring and all natural phenomena, offered no resistance to the new 'modern' imperialism and militarism.[16] The mental attitude of 'living in the now', of immediate unreflective action, proved fatally susceptible to the ideology of unquestioned submission to the will of the emperor. The colonising of the northern island of Hokkaido and the wars against China (1894-1895) and Russia (1904-1905), like the later invasion of Manchuria, thus acquired ideological legitimacy. To this day, especially in the light of resurgent nationalism and moves to revise the pacifist Article 9 of the post-war constitution, neither this militaristic past nor its Buddhist justification have been adequately addressed.

The Buddhist philosophers of the Kyoto School, who had attempted to utilise European philosophy in interpreting Buddhist teachings for the modern age, were completely disorientated by this political tendency to imperialism, torn back and forth between a deep loyalty to the Japanese nation and the Buddhist principles of equanimity and the overcoming of desire. The post-war generation, led by the 'critical Buddhists' Matsumoto Shiro

---

16   Victoria, Brian, *Zen at War* (New York/Tokyo: Weatherhill, 1997).

and Hakamaya Noriaki, sought the origins of this historic dead end in the falsification of the teachings of Indian Buddhism during its inculturation in China. Above all, the teachings of 'original enlightenment' (*hongaku shiso*) and the 'seed (or womb) of the Buddha-nature' (*tathagata garbha*) in all beings, which were derived from the supposedly Indian but actually Chinese scripture *The Awakening of Mahayana Faith,* were said to have misled Japanese Buddhists to adopt a substantialising and universalising of Buddhism, which allowed for an uncritical appropriation of the world as it is, including the gods and practices of Shinto. This acceptance of an underlying ontological 'place' (*dhatu*) was nothing other than the ancient Chinese nature mysticism in Buddhist dress. Everything, exactly as it is, is Buddha. This was the fatal conceptual error that misled even enlightened Zen masters to approve the imperial war policy.[17]

The role of Christianity in the modern history of Japan is extremely problematic.[18] If Buddhism, after undergoing centuries of inculturation since its introduction from China, could be regarded as 'foreign', how could Christianity, which was persecuted almost to the point of extermination for 200 years, be in any way at home in Japan? And how could its gospel of peace be credible in the light of the destruction of Hiroshima and Nagasaki by atomic bombs and of Tokyo by the firestorm of carpet bombing?

Nevertheless, there are remarkable examples of dialogue. A longstanding and philosophically profound conversation developed under the leadership of Abe Masao and John B. Cobb

---

17   Hakamaya, Noriaki, "Scholarship as Criticism", in: Jamie Hubbard und Paul L. Swanson, eds, *Pruning the Bodhi Tree: The Storm over Critical Buddhism* (Honolulu: University of Hawaii Press, 1997), 113-144; Matsumoto, Shiro, "The Meaning of 'Zen'", *ibid.* 242-250; in more detail May, *Transcendence and Violence,* 74-78.

18   Schmidt-Leukel, *Buddhist-Christian Relations in Asia,* Part IV, "Buddhist-Christian Relations in Japan".

between Buddhist philosophers and Christian theologians. The Kyoto philosophers have been the target of Buddhist critics, for whom their affinity with European phenomenology makes them vulnerable, but to an extent they have compensated for the failure of critical thinking under imperialism. Japanese Buddhist movements such as Soka Gakkai or Rissho Kosei-kai have shown that Buddhism can have global relevance when it returns to its sources (in this case the *Lotus-Sutra* and the prophetic thought of Nichiren, 1222-1282) and develops a humanistic ethic.

Significant peace initiatives, Buddhist in inspiration, have emerged in Vietnam (Thich Nhat Hanh), Cambodia (Goshananda), Thailand (Buddhadasa, Sulak Sivaraksa) and Sri Lanka (Ariaratne). In Myanmar and Sri Lanka, however, as we have observed, Buddhism has shown itself to be vulnerable to ethnically based nationalistic misappropriation. But the story of Buddhist resistance to exploitation and oppression shows that a Buddhist contribution to the discourse of global civil society in dialogue with Christianity is in the realm of possibility. Japan recovered from the moral and physical devastation of the war astonishingly quickly to become a leading economic power, but its spiritual energies have been smothered by the rampant material progress, its democratic structures are paralysed, and it has the greatest difficulty in admitting its war guilt to its Asian and Pacific neighbours.[19] Under pressure from the United States, in view of the threat from China and now North Korea, Japan would like to amend Article 9 of its post-war constitution, which states that "the Japanese people forever renounce war" (Paragraph 1), to make military action abroad possible once again. It is religious groups who are fighting this concession to the politics of the world powers.

---

19   McCormack, Gavan, *The Emptiness of Japanese Affluence* (St. Leonards: Allen & Unwin, 1996); May, *Transcendence and Violence*, 78-83.

4.3 Pacifism and the Religions

Ever since states have existed, conquest has been their *raison d'être*. Where does this leave the individual, and the religious tradition, opposed to violence? This, in a nutshell, is the pacifist dilemma. All the main religious traditions, to one degree or another, reject violence against humans and in some cases against all living beings. Yet again and again religions have been complicit in state-sponsored violence, occasioned by fear of foreigners or the urge to conquer territory. Whatever rationalisations have been employed to justify this, the fact remains that many religions provide grounds for rejecting violence in principle, i.e. for pacifism.

The early Buddhists, taking to heart the Buddha's teaching on nonduality and the interconnectedness of all beings, withdrew from active participation in the power-based politics of states and formed the alternative society of the *sangha* or community of monks (and, in the early centuries, of nuns). It therefore became a cultural expectation in Buddhist countries that monks were exempt from military service, though the laity had to find reasons for submitting to it despite the Buddha's precepts. The picture presented by history, of course, is very different, right up to the sanctioning of Japanese militarism and imperialism by Zen masters in Japan, the formation of a monks' political party to foster ethnic nationalism in Sri Lanka and the persecution of the Muslim Rohingya minority by Buddhists in Myanmar.[20]

The early Christians also faced this dilemma, but the story of how they dealt with it is not only instructive for the future history of pacifism, it reveals the origin of pacifism itself, properly

---

20 This and the following paragraphs are adapted from May, John D'Arcy, "Pacifism: Historical Phenomenon and Philosophical Problem", Norman Habel, ed., *Remembering Pioneer Australian Pacifist Charles Strong* (Northcote, Vic.: Morning Star, 2018), 41-54.

so called. It was inspired directly by the Christian Gospel; indeed, it characterised the stance of the church itself in the first three centuries. With long gaps in between, it re-emerged at various times in European Christian contexts, usually taking the form of a sectarian minority within or in opposition to established churches. But the reasons for its emergence and above all for its repeated decline are poorly understood. In its first three centuries to 313 CE, the infant church found its place in the harshly militaristic Roman world, in which war was taken for granted as the instrument of statecraft. There were Christian soldiers, though Christians tried to avoid accepting civil office because the state was seen as fundamentally evil; in particular, the military oath (*sacramentum*) recognised the emperor's deity and was therefore idolatrous. Instances of pacifism were sporadic and crystallised into an explicit stance only late.[21] Even before Constantine made Christianity the official imperial cult, loyalty to the state which did not involve idolatry was approved, and even after his ascension there was no abrupt *volte face*: Christians already became soldiers voluntarily.[22]

For the early Fathers such as Clement, Justin, Athenagoras and even Origen, military service does not appear to be an issue: "Christians could remain in the army as long as their role was non-violent";[23] but for Tertullian (160-220) it is incompatible with Christian faith, both because of the idolatry implicit in the military oath and the possibility of violence. Clement of Alexandria (150-215) saw Christians as belonging to a "bloodless army", though if they were soldiers they should obey commands; for Origen, they should support the emperor by prayer, not fighting, as killing is

---

21 See Nuttal, G.F., *Christian Pacifism in History* (Oxford: Blackwell, 1958), 2-3, 5-7, 9-10.
22 Swift, Louis J., ed., *The Early Fathers on War and Military Service* (Wilmington, Delaware: Glazier, 1983), 29-30, 80.
23 Swift, *Early Fathers*, 46.

forbidden.[24] "[W]hat seems to be developing in this period is an acknowledgement by pacifist writers that Christians may serve in the army provided they have nothing to do with bloodshed".[25]

Some writers, however, were unequivocal in their pacifism: "Killing a human being whom God willed to be inviolable is always wrong" (Lactantius, *Div. Inst.* 6.20.15-17); Swift comments: "This is pacifism pure and simple".[26] But it was also already a minority view and it foreshadows the paradoxes of pacifism which were to become more overt in later centuries. There were Christian soldiers who suffered martyrdom rather than continue to serve in Rome's armies, whereas the Constantinian apologist Eusebius of Caesarea (c. 260-c. 340) proclaimed a predestined harmony between Christian Church and Roman State. "[B]oth pacifist and non-pacifist positions existed side by side".[27] Acknowledging the legitimacy of the state entails approval of the use of necessary force, though this could be regarded as "sub-christian".[28]

The prevailing motive for refusing military service was *horror sanguinis*: it is always wrong to kill. Yet by 438 *only* Christians were permitted to serve.[29] By 340, in fact, "the older intransigence regarding military service was no longer workable".[30] St Basil (329-379) could proclaim the soldier a saint; for St Athanasius (296-373), military action did not amount to murder.[31] For St Ambrose (339-392), a Roman civil servant before he became bishop of Milan, Christian political responsibility sought "a middle ground

---

24 Swift, *Early Fathers,* 50, 52, 55-56.
25 Swift, *Early Fathers,* 59.
26 Swift, *Early Fathers,* 63.
27 Swift, *Early Fathers,* 79.
28 Brock, *Pacifism in Europe,* 18.
29 Brock, *Pacifism in Europe,* 24.
30 Swift, *Early Fathers,* 93.
31 Swift, *Early Fathers,* 94-95.

between uncritical acceptance of war and violence and a total relinquishing of statecraft".³² War against barbarians and heretics could be justified, though not for clergy or the church. War means untold misery, yet for St Augustine "the wise man will wage just wars ... for if they were not just he would not wage them" (*The City of God*, XIX.2).³³ The argument to justify war becomes strained: "violence and an internal spirit of love are not mutually exclusive", though only if legitimate authority decrees the use of force; private retaliation is excluded, whereas the soldier and the magistrate, who are not acting in their own interest, may resort to necessary violence.³⁴

The seeds of what was later to be known as the just war theory had already been sown. Violence in the service of a Christian empire is a duty, whether it is directed against internal or external threats. The fundamental ambivalence of just war theory lies in its attempt to justify the unjustifiable, the moral abomination that is war. Pacifism, as a principled stand against violence of any kind, has borne witness over the centuries to the unsustainability of just war theory. But in doing so it has condemned itself to being an idealistic stance, lacking political credibility.

It is not entirely true to say that pacifism is an exclusively Christian doctrine – the ancient Indian principle of *ahimsa*, literally unwillingness to harm any living creature, was as central to Gandhi as it had been to the Buddha – but the spectacle of Jesus' innocent suffering, regarded by the early Christians as the fulfilment of the Suffering Servant prophecy in Isaiah (Isaiah 50:4-9, 53:1-12), is the source of the Christian refusal to countenance physically harming others, political rationalisations notwithstanding. It is

---

32   Swift, *Early Fathers*, 97.
33   Augustine, Aurelius, *The City of God*, transl. Marcus Dods (New York: The Modern Library, 1950), 683.
34   Swift, *Early Fathers*, 123, 129, 134.

for this reason, perhaps, that pacifism was so often seen – and peremptorily dismissed – as a counsel of perfection, like chastity or voluntary poverty, admirable in those idealists who embraced it but politically non-viable. The emergence of a global civil society heralds the arrival of a new state of affairs in which the witness of pacifists may yet have political relevance.

Yet if even Buddhism, ostensibly the religion of peace and tolerance, allows itself to be drawn into the excesses we have seen in Sri Lanka and Myanmar, how is the religion's potential for peace to be made credible? In the canonical texts, Gautama Buddha is portrayed as a mediator in conflicts who lives by the ancient Indian teaching of *ahimsa* (unwillingness to harm any living being). The entire basis of his teaching (*dhamma*) consists in the rooting out of the threefold cause of violence: greed (*lobha*), hatred (*dosa*) and delusion (*moha*). One can only conclude that in this respect the religions are ambivalent: they contain within themselves noble teachings on peace, but all too easily they let themselves be won over to ethnically, culturally and economically motivated violence.[35]

In the context of a global civil society wracked by conflicts ostensibly motivated by religion, such ambivalence is dangerous. The relations between religion and politics are extremely complex and must be better understood if the religions are plausibly to present themselves as factors in peacebuilding rather than causes of conflict. The attitudes of the so-called 'Abrahamic' or monotheistic religions – Judaism, Christianity and Islam – to violence and peace must be honestly – and if possible, collaboratively – brought to

---

35 Appleby, R. Scott, *The Ambivalence of the Sacred: Religion, Violence, and Reconciliation* (Lanham, Md.: Rowman & Littlefield, 2000); May, *Transcendence and Violence*, 148-154.

light.[36] But the great Asian traditions – Hinduism, Buddhism and Confucianism – have shown themselves to be equally capable of radicalisation and aggression. Working through these problems together is perhaps *the* ecumenical task posed by the emerging global civil society.

---

36   This task has been taken in hand in a thorough study by Stobbe, Heinz-Günther, *Religion, Gewalt und Krieg. Eine Einführung* (Stuttgart: Kohlhammer, 2010).

Chapter 5: Land and Life as Religious Values

(Australia and Melanesia)

The idea that land could be anything else than property, the object of buying and selling, is alien to the Western mind. Land is there to be used, exploited, as the site of agriculture, forestry or mining. Whoever neglects to *use* land, whether to build a house on it or enjoy it aesthetically as 'landscape', forfeits any right to it. So-called traditional or indigenous peoples have an entirely different relationship to land, ignorance of which led to many a misunderstanding between them and European settlers. For them, land is the source of life itself, and, as the 'place' where individual and tribe took their origin, it is sacred. The earth in which a people is rooted is at the same time an inheritance, with which the mythical narratives of ancestors and culture heroes are interwoven. The right to use land can be negotiated, but never its actual possession. The people are possessed by the land, not the other way around. The main responsibility of the community, and of the individual towards the community, is the prudent use and protection of the land for the continuity of life. Even the dead are incorporated into this community: they are part of the meta-community to which all, living and dead, belong.[1]

For Australia's original inhabitants, the natural features, which Europeans call 'landscape' and enjoy as tourists, are concretisations of the 'Dreaming', the 'every-when' (Stanner), a time beyond all time in which the 'abiding events' (Tony Swain) that shape the land took place and continue to take place. As these

---

1 Gesch, Patrick V., *Initiative and Initiation: A Cargo Cult-Type Movement in the Sepik Against Its Background in Traditional Village Religion* (St. Augustin: Anthropos-Institut, 1985).

cultural relationships pervade the entire Asia-Pacific in different ways, it is fundamentally important for our project to understand their deeper meaning and their relationship to Western and Asian understandings of religion. We will thus need to study so-called 'primal religion' in two of its manifestations, first in Australia (5.1) and then in Melanesia (5.2), before moving on to look at the implications of this phenomenon for the 'higher' world religions, the global economy and global communication (5.3).

5.1 Land as the Presence of Spirit: The Aborigines

There is a correlation between the geographical conditions in which people live and their ways of believing. The desert is the place where the great monotheistic religions originated, the jungle is the home of religions based on nature, though this is, of course, an over-simplification: too late it was recognised that Australian Aboriginal religion has a profound sense of the transcendent, while Melanesian cultures, though not theistic, have community-promoting rituals that can only be called religious. In the case of the Aborigines, and in aspects of the Melanesian and Polynesian cultures of Pacific Islanders, we find a spiritual life which – not unlike the closeness to nature of Japanese Shinto – long remained hidden from the invading Europeans, because it is fundamentally bound up with a deep relationship to land as a life-giving 'place' ('country' in Australia) suffused with meaning. The word 'religion' suggests a relationship (*re-ligare*) to life's central, most important value; to this extent, this relationship to land as the determinate 'place' from which life springs is religious, and in more recent times Europeans have discovered in it a spirituality which complements the more abstract teachings of Christianity.[2]

---

2   Stockton, Eugene, *The Aboriginal Gift: Spirituality for a Nation* (Alexandria, NSW: Millennium Books, 1995); see also Appendix 1, Ungunmerr, Miriam

The British soldiers and their prisoners found their first encounter with the Great South Land profoundly alienating and disturbing. Everything was different: the animals that fled jumping on their hind legs; the birds that laughed cheekily at the invaders; the trees whose grey-green leaves were always the same; and the dark forms that flitted through the bush and could have been human beings. Clashes were inevitable, because the new arrivals, relying completely on their own meagre resources, urgently needed to learn how to survive in the dried-out bushland around Port Jackson; in other words: they needed land.

They had the greatest difficulty in seeing the original inhabitants as human at all; in any case, it was clear that they had no conception of doing anything useful with the land. So the whites lost no time building houses, putting up fences, grazing cattle and, above all, making sure to secure water sources. They had not the slightest inkling of the Aborigines' needs, which were not only material but spiritual: the places appropriated by the whites for their own use were important not just for physical survival but for the sacred ceremonies that ensured it. The first fatalities probably occurred when white settlers shot Aborigines who were trying to gain access to their traditional waterholes and ceremonial grounds and in the attempt killed sheep and cattle and trespassed on the newly-fenced fields. Two worlds which could hardly have been more different came into conflict in what Stockton calls "the most severe culture clash in history".[3]

What the Europeans failed to grasp was that the Aborigines had a deep emotional and spiritual relationship to particular places which were sacred to them for deeply religious reasons. The

---

Rose, "*Dadirri*", 179-184; Stockton, "Eine erd-gesinnte Spiritualität im heutigen Australien", Hans Kessler, ed., *Ökologisches Weltethos im Dialog der Kulturen und Religionen* (Darmstadt: Wissenschaftliche Buchgesellschaft, 1996), 183-195.

3   Stockton, *Aboriginal Gift*, 18.

various peoples were eternally bound to these areas by language and song, story and custom. They were often on the move, which irritated the whites; but their paths were precisely determined by the 'songlines', the song cycles that gave these localities meaning, 'sang them into being' and mapped them for those who moved through them. To be separated from these places amounted to cultural and eventually physical death. Their resistance to white invasion, which was much stronger than the historiography of the victors admitted, was at the same time literally a life and death struggle.

I have long been aware that in Western Victoria, where I grew up, there is evidence of Aboriginal villages consisting of substantial stone houses and sustained by ingenious fish and eel traps. These people were thus not simply 'hunter-gatherers', as conventional anthropology maintained. More recent research has shown that Aboriginal civilisation throughout the continent was based on highly sophisticated agricultural techniques which could rightly be called 'farming', the cultivation and storage of grains and tubers suited to dry environments in landscapes shaped by the judicious use of fire to control excess growth, facilitate hunting and stimulate germination.[4] The remains now being uncovered point to the extreme antiquity of these practices, possibly exceeding 80,000 years.

How the abundant evidence of a sedentary agricultural and acquacultural way of life perfectly adapted to harsh conditions disappeared so quickly from the historical record and the

---

4   Gammage, Bill, *The Biggest Estate on Earth: How Aborigines Made Australia* (Sydney: Allen & Unwin, 2012); Pascoe, Bruce, *Dark Emu: Aboriginal Australia and the Birth of Agriculture* (Broome: Magabala Books, rev. ed. 2018). Both draw on the journals and letters of the first white settlers and explorers, which contain overwhelming evidence of land management radically different from that introduced by Europeans. Some of their conclusions are necessarily speculative, and Gammage defends his against critics in a lengthy Appendix.

consciousness of Australians is something of a mystery. It can only be explained by the colonisers' desire to suppress any evidence of the natives' humanity and ingenuity in favour of the invidious doctrine of *terra nullius*: the land was so untouched by human culture and industry as to be effectively unoccupied. Pascoe cites many examples of otherwise sympathetic explorers noting with astonishment the ways in which Aborigines managed fish stocks, ground grain and built comfortable houses, but immediately going on to comment on how suitable the land would be for European crops and livestock. The thoughtless introduction of sheep and cattle soon all but eliminated the native grasses and wreaked havoc on the fragile soils so carefully cultivated by the Aborigines. Their ways of using the land were intimately bound up with the spiritual vision of the Dreaming, and Pascoe even muses that their social structures may have resembled what we call 'democracy': "Of all the systems humans have devised to manage their lives on earth, Aboriginal government looks most like the democratic model".[5]

The whites' fundamental misunderstanding of Indigenous culture has weighed on relations between the Aborigines and all subsequent waves of immigration. The British settlers were at least nominally Protestant Christians, and not a few protested about the hunting down of Aborigines. The Benedictine Archbishop Polding publicly defended their rights as human beings with immortal souls. A discussion ensued which some believe was the most important in Australian history, and it continues to this day.[6] The pragmatic, rationalistic mentality of present-day Australians, reinforced by militant atheism and secularism, is blind to both: the spiritual side of indigenous culture with its intuition into

---

5   Pascoe, *Dark Emu*, 187.
6   Fletcher, Frank, *Jesus and the Dreaming: Discovering an Australian Spirituality Through Aboriginal-Christian Dialogue* (Strathfield: St Pauls Publications, 2013), 236; see also May, *Transcendence and Violence,* Chapter 1.

the meaning of land, and the mystical side of Christian faith, which leads us far beyond dogmas and morals.[7] The historian of Australian religious thought, Wayne Hudson, goes so far as to say: "At times Aboriginal identification with their own spirituality as the spirituality of the land was strong enough to rival the parareligious discourse of Anzac Day".[8]

One of the primary expressions of Aboriginal spirituality is the mythic symbol of the Dreaming, the not uncontroversial translation of the word *alcheringa* from the Arrente language of central Australia, which can also mean Law. In this transcendent dimension of the natural world, the ancestors timelessly perform the deeds that are forever immanent in features of the land as 'abiding events'.[9] The rites traditionally carried out repeatedly at these sacred places made possible a participation in the mythical events which has been called 'sacramental'.[10] In this regard, it is by no means exaggerated when Aborigines declare that the land that bore them and nourished them 'cries out' and 'weeps' when it is stripped bare by huge herds of cattle and flocks of sheep and disfigured by iron ore, coal and bauxite mines.

Thanks to a judgment of the High Court, they now have a say in the way their land is exploited, as long as they can prove that particular places have been continually used for ritual purposes. This legal formality appears incongruous in the light of the evidence

---

[7] Fletcher, *Jesus and the Dreaming*, 101.

[8] Hudson, Wayne, *Australian Religious Thought* (Clayton, Vic.: Monash University Publishing, 2016), 231; see 183-194.

[9] Swain, Tony, *A Place for Strangers: Towards a History of Aboriginal Being* (Cambridge: Cambridge University Press, 1993). There are a number of other words with similar meanings, e.g. *tjukurrpa*; Stockton occasionally translates them with 'Dreaming Ones'.

[10] Wilson, Martin, *New, Old and Timeless: Pointers Toward an Aboriginal Theology* (Kensingon: Chevalier Press, 1979), following the anthropologist W. E. H. Stanner, who had an exceptional appreciation of the religious dimension of Aboriginal culture.

cited earlier that Aborigines in fact husbanded and cultivated the entire continent for millennia. In its 1992 judgment, the High Court found in favour of Eddie Koiki Mabo of Murray Island in the Torres Strait, who had claimed that his land belonged to him by virtue of unbroken possession and ritual use. This meant that the principle of *terra nullius* (at the time of colonisation the land belonged to 'no-one', because the Aborigines had no legal status) was abrogated, and the principle of native title was confirmed.

But things were not that simple. A later judgment (in a case brought by the Wik people of north Queensland in 1996) determined that, where a conflict arises, native title yields to the claims of the large pastoral and mining interests, though both can co-exist. In order to extinguish native title, however, this intention must be explicitly contained in the law invoked by the government or the farmers. Factually and legally, nevertheless, the Mabo judgment was undermined, as laws proposed in 1998, 2009 and 2014 confirm. The original legislation of 1994, as a result of Mabo, was undoubtedly revolutionary, in that the validity of indigenous, religiously founded land rights was recognised in British-based Australian law, but ultimately it served to control native title rather than establish it.

The procedure of establishing native title by means of archaeological and anthropological evidence is lengthy and expensive. The Christian churches had to overcome determined political opposition to prepare the ground for these judgments and ensure that they became law.[11] Nevertheless, four times more land rights cases have been successful than were rejected. On 13 March 2019, the High Court awarded the Ngaliwurru and Nungali peoples of Timber Creek reduced compensation for the

---

11   Williamson, Raymond K., *Pilgrims of Hope: An Ecumenical Journey 1980-2010* (Northcote: Morning Star Publishing, 2014), Chapter 8, gives an exhaustive account of these efforts.

economic value of their land, but upheld their compensation claim for its cultural value, distinguishing clearly for the first time between economic and spiritual criteria.

The land calls to mind the abiding events of archaic time, eternally present in the rituals and symbolised as the Dreaming. What this amounts to is an unbroken web of meanings spanning the entire continent. It contains and bears witness to a treasure trove of laws, languages and stories.[12] Forcible separation from the land has often enough extinguished the memory of these cultural treasures, but Aboriginal people still carry within themselves the ceremonies that define their identity, concealed from the gaze of uncomprehending whites. In the cities, a 'New Dreaming' has come into being which no longer regards only the relationship to particular places as sacred, but *that* and *how* relationship to country persists, finding new expression in the outstanding artistic creations of Aborigines.[13] This relationship to land as the original defining 'place' of identity is something every human being can appreciate. Christians may see in it a trace of 'pagan' nature religion, forgetting that the land is an absolutely central theme of the Hebrew Bible, even if in Christian faith and theology the human relationship to the earth as creation and 'nature' plays only a subordinate role.[14]

Christians who have engaged with this religious dimension of Aboriginal culture discover a cosmic spirituality that nourishes their faith in unexpected ways. They learn to listen silently and

---

12 Fletcher, *Jesus and the Dreaming*, 223.

13 Swain, Tony, "Reinventing the Eternal: Aboriginal Spirituality and Modernity", Norman C. Habel, ed., *Religion and Multiculturalism in Australia: Essays in Honour of Victor Hayes* (Adelaide: Australian Association for the Study of Religions, 1992), 122-136, 130.

14 May, John D'Arcy, "Rootedness: Reflections on Land and Belonging", Werner Jeanrond and Andrew D. H. Mays, eds, *Recognising the Margins: Developments in Biblical and Theological Studies. Essays in Honour of Seán Freyne* (Dublin: Columba Press, 2006), 146-159.

intently (*dadirri*) to the 'speaking land',[15] to see creation as primal revelation, to decipher the land as a metaphor for the mystical. Although just about everything in contemporary Australian culture, dominated by technology and profit-making, seems to work against it, this encounter of two religious worlds in the deeper levels of Australian consciousness is happening. Christians themselves are converted, not directly to the cosmic spirituality of the Aborigines, but to a wider interpretation of their own faith. They discover the wholeness of creation, from the depths of the human soul to the hidden secrets of the natural world, irrespective of practical purposes and rational calculus.[16] Herein they have the basis for an ethic that allows them to see clearly the appalling social problems with which Aborigines are confronted: alcohol, drugs, unemployment, family breakdown. On all criteria – health care, life expectancy, incarceration rates, suicide, alcohol and drug abuse – the Aborigines are far above the national average.

Unlike Canada or New Zealand, Australia still has no formal treaty with its Aboriginal peoples which would enshrine their status as 'first nations' in the constitution, where their 40,000 (possibly 80,000) year history in the land is not even mentioned, though in 1967 a referendum granted them the right to vote. Despite the apology offered by prime minister Kevin Rudd on behalf of all Australians in 2008, all subsequent efforts to 'close the gap' have made painfully slow progress. A long hard road lies ahead until the original inhabitants of the continent receive the genuine reconciliation and legal recognition that is their due.

---

15   Berndt, Ronald M., and Catherine H. Berndt, *The Speaking Land: Myth and Story in Aboriginal Australia* (Ringwood: Penguin, 1988), see Ungunmerr, Miriam Rose, "*Dadirri*", Stockton, Eugene, *The Aboriginal Gift: Spirituality for a Nation* (Alexandria, NSW: Millennium Books, 1995), Appendix 1, 179-184.

16   Fletcher, *Jesus and the Dreaming*, referring to Tacey, David, *Edge of the Sacred: Transformation in Australia* (Melbourne: HarperCollins, 1995).

5.2 Wellbeing and Community: The Melanesians

In every society at least three factors determine the ways people live together. *Homo sapiens* is above all *homo habilis*: the fashioning of tools and weapons creates the possibility of producing food and clothing, thus ensuring survival. But in order to achieve this, people's social relationships – especially sexual relations, on which reproduction depends – must be regulated in such a way that all share the tasks that contribute to the wellbeing of all. What finally differentiates humans from animals, however, is the construction of a web of meanings, which makes all these arrangements appear justified, right and given. Precisely, this is a *social* achievement. With this, culture – the taboos that regulate the hunt, the rituals that accompany gardening and harvest – passes over into cult, a 'religious' practice, though with little or no relationship to what the great religious systems would identify as religious. Meanings are created and transmitted in order that the social activities on which life and livelihood depend 'make sense' and are proof against deviation and abuse. This collusion of the three dimensions can be represented schematically thus:

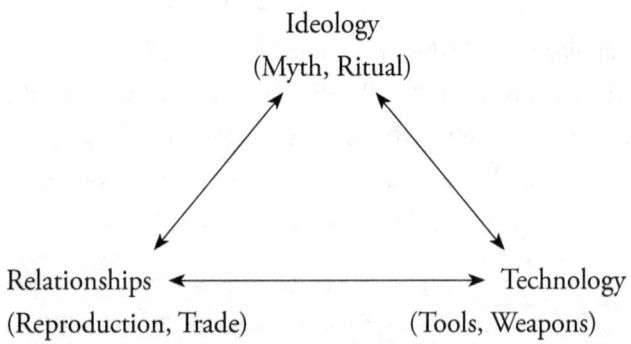

Even societies that appear to be stable over long periods of time undergo change, whether it is because of climate change, new inventions or encounters with other peoples and their different stories and customs. It only needs one of the three factors to change in order to modify the other two: novel tools and weapons must be sanctioned by the ancestors or the gods; new social structures or division of labour affect the work rhythms of society; new myths, whether imposed by invaders or adopted from neighbouring peoples, suggest new ways of ordering the network of social relationships. Society and community are practically identical; all social behaviour is laid down in advance.

'Religion', then, in the context of such societies, is not an abstraction which is imposed from above or from without, but is the cohesion of all areas of life in the everyday world. We need not be surprised, therefore, that the religious ideas of the desert-dwelling societies of Australia look different from those of the jungle-dwelling peoples of New Guinea. These seem to have discovered gardening independently of other civilisations some 9000 years ago, although as we have seen the Australians practised agricultural techniques many millennia earlier. Mircea Eliade called this epoch-making breakthrough to the growing and storage of food 'the longest revolution', because it made possible a settled life in one place through the whole year. From similar beginnings elsewhere grew cities and states with their accompanying ideological and political structures. Agriculture, the unlocking of the fruitfulness of the earth under cultivation by particular groups of people, became the source of the metaphors and symbols which underlie the myths of the creation of life, the earth and the cosmos. To this extent, the land and its cultivation form the basis of religious language itself.

The whole of life and the cycle of life, including hunting, gardening and reproduction, must be kept in balance. Agriculture, the shaping of the land and the domestication of animals to bring forth the produce that sustains life, and the economy in the sense of the distribution and exchange of goods, all belong in this thoroughly religious context. If it is true that archaic cultures based on hunting and keeping animals adopted an attitude of thankfulness towards a more-than-human giver of life, which was expressed in the primitial offering of the first-born or the first fruits of the earth, then traces of this theism survived in the 'biocosmic' religion of those who invented agriculture, the cultivation of the earth to produce edible fruits at predictable times.[17] Schematically, one could say that desert peoples developed a 'vertical' relationship to the sacred, which led to the birth of the great monotheistic religions, whereas the religion of gardeners was 'horizontal', lived out in the 'meta-society' of relationships among the members of the tribe, with the surrounding peoples and the spirits of the ancestors (*tumbuna*) and nature (*masalai*).

In Melanesia, the wellbeing of (one's own) community (*gutpela sindaun*, 'sitting down together in peace and prosperity') is a fundamental ethical value that determines everything else in the life of the community and the individual. The relationship to tribal land, which provides nourishment and secures and symbolises the continuity of life itself, is thus an ethical one. What matters are the activities that guard this land and its use, whether in exchange relations with neighbours, the conduct of war against them or in the resolution of conflicts within the community. Not abstract truth, but concrete effectiveness is the pragmatic criterion according to which technologies and the mythic concepts that sanction them are judged.

In Melanesian languages, there is no word for 'apologise': if one wishes to make good an offence, one must *act* and restore

---

[17] This is a central theme in Mantovani, Ennio, *The Dema and the Christ: My Engagement and Inner Dialogue with the Cultures and Religions of Melanesia* (Siegburg: Franz Schmitt Verlag, 2014).

the balance with a gift; similarly, there is no word for 'thank': the giving itself makes good the debt. The most highly regarded religious act was traditionally the organisation of a generous feast by the clan leader, the *bikman* ('big man'), who demonstrated his status by showing that he had the resources at his disposal to distribute gifts to all. The greatest example was the now defunct pig festival, which was prepared over a long period of time so that as many pigs as possible could be slaughtered and distributed according to the political priorities of the organiser. It took a long time for Christian missionaries to grasp that this was a kind of eucharist, a 'giving thanks' in the form of a communal action which represented death as the source of life.[18]

The mythical narrative that framed such cultic acts in many parts of Melanesia was the ritual killing of a being – a brother, sometimes a woman – so that the land would become fruitful once again. These culture heroes were called *dema*, and although their death was sometimes understood as sacrifice, it seems rather that it was a kind of exchange: in return for the life of the *dema* new life sprang forth.[19] It is understandable that the first missionaries had great difficulty interpreting these phenomena as in any way 'religious', no doubt because this thoroughgoing embedding of the human in nature was alien to them. This was not theism, but what Mantovani calls 'biocosmic' religion, in which physical life itself is the *religious* value overriding all others. "If the Melanesians seemed to exaggerate the material aspect of salvation, Christians were exaggerating the spiritual one".[20] At the same time, there was

---

18   Mantovani, *The Dema and the Christ*, 116-123.
19   Mantovani, *The Dema and the Christ*, discusses the possible theological significance of this cult extensively, rejecting the interpretation of Theodor Ahrens that he is clandestinely introducing the idea of 'sacrifice' into this exchange by terming it a 'memorial'; see May, *Transcendence and Violence*, 58.
20   Mantovani, *The Dema and the Christ*, 191, see 100.

an ever-present awareness of a 'more-than-human' giver of all the gifts of nature and life itself.[21]

5.3 Land as the Basis of Interreligious Communication

It is difficult for the Western Christian believer or theologian to conceive of the basis of interreligious relations other than as abstract and conceptual. The reason, perhaps, is that the Western way of thinking gives priority to the individual, whereas "[i]n the Melanesian world view there is no individual in the Western sense. One exists because one belongs to a community… For Melanesians, relationships give more than identity: they create a person".[22] What counts is community, and as the individual only survives by being embedded in the community, he or she is thought of in an entirely different way. Put very briefly: in the Western understanding the ego with its body is distinct from nature:

Self-body / world

The Melanesian view, on the other hand, is that the ego is socially constituted by participating in a world that includes the body:

Self / body-world

In this scheme of things, it becomes evident how incidental one's own ego can be in such a society: it is constituted entirely by the manifold relationships to the world of nature as prescribed by the community; "the self regards the body as an incidental support for life itself, which continues after physical death and consists in

---

21 Mantovani, *The Dema and the Christ*, 56-59.
22 Mantovani, *The Dema and the Christ*, 196.

a many-sided network of relationships".[23]

> The chief, as the personification of the ancestral line and its authority, represents security by presiding over the circulation of gifts and safeguarding the narrative in which the tradition is embodied. The *ego* stands in relationship with the totem, the spirit ancestor, the uterine group, and the mysterious powers of passion: it is this complex that constitutes mythic time and the existence of the individual... It is thus that tradition and myth are able to comprehend the whole of existence over generations.[24]

The living person, the *kamo*, "exists only to the extent that it exercises its role within the play of these relationships".[25] This spirituality of 'body-in-nature' shocked the early Christian missionaries. When Leenhardt suggested to an acquaintance in New Caledonia that Christianity must have given people there a sense of the spiritual, the reply was: "No, not at all, we always had that; what you brought us was the body".[26] "In other words, the breaking of the body-nature continuum revealed the body as an object vis-à-vis the person, a hindrance to self-development rather than its instrument, indeed as a source of moral danger, something

---

23 Hogan, Linda, and John D'Arcy May, "Constructing the Human: Dignity in Interreligious Dialogue", *The Discourse of Human Dignity. Concilium* 39/2 (2003), 78-89, 81.

24 Hogan and May, "Constructing the Human", 81, paraphrasing Leenhardt; see next footnote.

25 Leenhardt, Maurice, *Do Kamo. La personne et le mythe dans le monde mélanésien* (Paris: Gallimard, [1947] 1971), 249.

26 Ahrens, Theodor, "'Was ihr uns gebracht habt ist der Körper'. Erwägungen zur Frage, was Missionswissenschaft zur Erkenntnis Gottes beiträgt", unpubl. manuscript, 13-17; *id.*, *Mission nachdenken. Studien* (Frankfurt: Lembeck, 2002), 161-165.

quite alien to indigenous culture".[27] Equally alien was the notion that there are 'religions', among which the individual may choose after ranking them according to their value and relevance for his or her own life.

The Western approach, which starts with the needs of the individual and objectifies the values embodied in the religions in the light of them, is different. Aspects of a particular religion must be generalised and universalised in order to be compared with those of another religion. In this way, a frame of reference is constructed within which the two faiths can encounter one another (we shall return to this question in 8.1 below). What is lacking in this conception is the sense that *every* religion, even those that claim absolute truth and universal validity, has taken its rise from some *place*, whose climate, topography, imagery and culture leave their impress on it, even when it seeks to put down roots in another context. Buddhism, perhaps, comes to terms most easily with the necessity of adapting itself to local conditions if it is to survive outside India; Islam seems least able to do so. Christianity, as a result of its long missionary history, has grappled intensively with the problem of the limits of inculturation where it comes into contact with worldviews and customs that deviate markedly from its own.

In every case, these are bound up with the relationship to the earth as land, as a *place* fraught with meaning, without which even the putatively most transcendent of religions could not subsist. To put it briefly: the 'metacosmic' religions of transcendence would dissolve into thin air if they did not appropriate as their foundation

---

27   Hogan, Linda, und John D'Arcy May, "Gender and Culture as Dimensions of Bodiliness", Harm Goris, ed., *Bodiliness and Human Dignity: An Intercultural Approach / Leiblichkeit und Menschenwürde. Interkulturelle Zugänge* (Berlin: LIT Verlag, 2006), 45-57, 54.

the 'biocosmic' religion that propagates and celebrates life.[28] For the 'universal' faiths, the latter is often regarded as 'pagan', 'materialistic' nature religion; but wherever humans are religious – and that is pretty well everywhere, apart from the secularised West – they are religious in this way. As Mantovani rightly remarks, "The most important aspect of a primal religion… is that it provides the building blocks to the universal religions".[29]

It follows that interreligious communication, not least in a global civil society, has as its foundation this dimension of the 'primal' religion of land and life. Comparative religion, as religious studies was formerly called, has provided a wealth of material from which to reconstruct this level of communication. The metaphors that are the wellspring of all language, especially religious language, are drawn in the first place from nature and the human relationship to nature, as in the similes and parables of the Gospels, the Buddhist canon and the Qur'an. From them derives the symbolism that forms the linguistic underpinning of teachings and ethical values. I call these 'primary' and 'secondary' symbolisation. Once we have understood this relationship, we can more easily appreciate how religious language functions. It is more akin to poetry than philosophy and has its own criteria of truth.

In the fluid situation of communication in global civil society, it will be important to pay attention to these relationships. The status of religious symbols changes once they stand alongside one another and flow into each other. This is not to imply 'syncretism' or 'relativism', but rather a kind of linguistic osmosis, a mutual

---

28   These concepts, developed by Aloysius Pieris and Ennio Mantovani respectively, have been helpful in my own research; see May, John D'Arcy, *Transcendence and Violence: The Encounter of Buddhist, Christian and Primal Traditions* (London & New York: Continuum, 2003); May, John D'Arcy, *Christus Initiator. Theologie im Pazifik* (Düsseldorf: Patmos, 1990 = Theologie Interkulturell 4).

29   Mantovani, *The Dema and the Christ*, 187.

appropriation of others' religious symbols in order to express one's own doctrines better. In this new kind of symphony – sometimes cacophony – of meanings, all speakers stand on the common ground of the one earth, even when they develop the most abstract concepts in order to distance themselves from it by generalisation. The relationship to the 'earthed' religions, the 'little' traditions of earth's island, desert and mountain peoples is especially important for assessing the validity of ethical values.

Chapter 6: Economic Ethics: Globalising Values?

(Melanesia and Thailand)

We may be forgiven for thinking that 'economic ethics' is a Western concept, of Christian inspiration. Are there Buddhist economic ethics, or Islamic, or Confucian? How would they be distinguished from one another? To ask this is to question things Westerners take for granted: do these alternative meaning contexts include what we would call objective norms or universal validity, which we regard as criteria for a functioning economy? Trade is as old as humanity itself, and ancient civilisations originally created writing and numbers in order to have a reliable basis for their business dealings, which could thus be quantified, expressed in numbers and objectively described. But capitalism – first financial, then industrial – is an invention of modernity, first in late Medieval Europe, then as the driving force in the opening up of America for European settlement, and now in the even more spectacular modernisation of Asia. Do the much quoted, but seldom defined, 'Asian values' make for a different kind of economic development in the Asia-Pacific?

The response to the destructive individualism of profit-hungry capitalism was the equally European ideology of socialism, which, however, did not, as foreseen by Marx and Engels, take root in the working classes of the industrialised nations but among those of the agriculturally based societies of Russia and China. Neither system succeeded in its aims. Socialism was only able to be maintained by dictatorships, even if they were theoretically dictatorships of the proletariat, and they were institutionalised as *state* socialism; and capitalism, just as Marx prophesied, staggers from crisis to crisis, while the poor become poorer and the rich become ever richer. This has been well characterised as 'casino capitalism', arcane systems of speculation designed to make money out of other people's money, with the stock market as its barometer of greed.

A conventional estimate illustrates this with a champagne glass: the top 20 per cent (the bowl) claim 82 per cent of the world's wealth, while only 1.4 per cent remains for the bottom 20 per cent (the base).[1] More recently, the *World Inequality Report* gives a more differentiated analysis: global inequality is growing steadily, but at widely varying rates in different parts of the world. In the Middle East, the top 10 per cent of income earners hold an astonishing 61 per cent of the wealth; in the case of India, the figure stands at 55 per cent; in Russia 46 per cent; in China 41 per cent; but in Europe only 37 per cent.

In most countries, there have been substantial transfers of public wealth to private ownership since 1980. While the top 1 per cent shared close to 10 per cent of national income in both Europe and the US at that time, by 2016 it had risen to 12 per cent in Western Europe, but reached 20 per cent in the US. Worldwide, the top 1 per cent wealthiest individuals owned 33 per cent of total wealth in 2017; the bottom 50 per cent of the population owns less than 2 per cent of wealth over the same period since 1980. The increase was most marked in the top 0.1 per cent of income earners in the US.[2] Economy properly so called is the humane regulation

---

[1] Houtart, François, *Délégitimer le capitalisme. Reconstruire l'espérance* (Brüssel: Editions Colophon, 2005); Houtart, François, and François Polet, *The Other Davos: Globalization of Resistances and Struggles* (Tiruvalla: Christava Sahitya Samithi, 2000).

[2] I am indebted to Dr Bruce Duncan for drawing my attention to the *World Inequality Report* and to an article by Antonio Savola, "Global inequality is on the rise – but at vastly different rates across the world", in *The Conversation*, 14/12/2017.

of the whole household (from *oikos*, 'house'); as the theory behind these staggering figures, it has been reduced to chrematistics, from the Greek word for mere accounting, gambling on hypothetical values instead of trading the actual worth of goods and services.[3]

Having looked in the previous chapter at the way ethical values arise out of concrete relationships to land and life, we must now pursue the question that occupied Max Weber: where do the values that underlie an economy come from? Do ethical values necessarily have a religious foundation? If so, how can it be shown that ethical values regulate economic activity according to the religious values from which they derive? And does either set of values determine the social context of economic activity? Can such values then be transferred to completely different cultures in the course of globalisation?

Two examples immediately come to mind: China, deeply influenced by the hierarchical and family orientated value system of Confucianism, as can be seen wherever in the world the Chinese do business, now seeks to draw level with the United States economically and militarily; and Japan, which, after the failed attempt to establish a 'Greater East Asia Co-Prosperity Sphere' by conquest and exploitation of neighbouring countries during the Second World War, came to terms with the democratic constitution prescribed by the Americans and rose to become a global economic power. The imperial dynasty was deprived of its divine status but not abolished, so that the founding myth remained as the expression of a strong national sentiment, though the significance of the ancient Japanese religion for the country's astonishing industrial development is not easy to gauge.

---

3   Cobb, John B., and Herman Daly, *For the Common Good: Redirecting the Economy toward Community, the Environment and a Sustainable Future* (Boston: Beacon Press, 1989); May, John D'Arcy, "Die ökumenische Alternative. Die eine bewohnte Erde neu denken", *Salzburger Theologische Zeitschrift* 14/2 (2010), 187-202.

Although Buddhism has inspired socially engaged lay movements such as Rissho Kosei-kai and, in the case of Soka Gakkai, even a political party, the Komeitai, its role is seen as otherworldly and is largely restricted to honouring the *kami* of the dead, while Shinto celebrates the relationship to the natural world.

The outcome of the Japanese experiment with capitalism – not unlike China's experience with socialism – is a meaning vacuum, a spiritual deficit, an inner emptiness that is only partially filled by rapid economic development.[4] It remains to be seen whether and how the mythic substratum of economic activity and theory influences economic practice. It could well be that economics is not the value-neutral positive science as which it is conventionally understood, but a much larger narrative about the good life, a normative discipline drawing on ancient myths to which it has become oblivious.[5] In what follows, we shall undertake two case studies which may shed light on these aspects of economic ethics: the exchange economy using the products of nature in the Pacific Islands (6.1) and the economic significance of transcendent values in Buddhism (6.2). On this basis, we may then gain a better understanding of the relationship between the globalisation of the world economy and the globalisation of ethical and religious values in global civil society (6.3).

6.1 Reciprocity and Retribution in Melanesia

The basis of all economic activity in the traditional societies of the South Pacific is land, complemented in coastal areas by the sea, as the source of all life. It is one's relationship to some piece

---

4   McCormack, Gavan, *The Emptiness of Japanese Affluence* (St Leonards: Allen & Unwin, 1996).

5   Sedlacek, Thomas, *Economics of Good and Evil: The Quest for Economic Meaning from Gilgamesh to Wall Street* (New York: Oxford University Press, 2011). We shall return to this fascinating study below.

of earth that first makes one human; whoever has no right to land is a *rabisman* (rubbish, worth nothing). This relationship does not consist of legal possession, as in the West, but is the right to use land conferred by the social group (clan, tribe, people), and is thus more a duty than a right. Life in its most comprehensive sense, flowing forth from land and sea, is the central religious value, and all trade with the fruits of nature and the activities that produce them – gardening, fishing, hunting – takes place strictly in ritual contexts.

In Melanesia, whatever is exchanged – women, pigs, fruits, game, decorations, in some cases shell money – serves to increase the wealth of the *bikman*, but this does not simply mean personal enrichment: a great reserve of pigs, bananas, fish, etc., together with the fertility of women and gardens, was traditionally the basis for the great festivals which confirmed the status of the *bikman* and bound the members of the group to him more firmly. All such largesse must be repaid, if possible even more generously, so that the former host and benefactor once again becomes a debtor.[6]

This is the iron law of payback (*bekim*, restitution, retribution), which always holds irrespective of Western institutions such as courts or insurances. In Melanesian languages, as we saw, there is usually no word for 'thanks' or 'apology': only deeds count. "Gifts are silent words… it is not enough to say 'I'm sorry'. Instead, one must 'do sorry', which is to say, 'do something'".[7] Good and evil are paid back, with interest. In the first instance, one's loyalty is to the family, the clan, the members of one's own people (*wantoks*, 'one-talks', i.e. our people, who speak our language – especially

---

6   May, John D'Arcy, *Christus Initiator. Theologie im Pazifik* (Düsseldorf: Patmos, 1990 = Theologie Interkulturell 4), Chapter 4.

7   Mantovani, Ennio, *The Dema and the Christ: My Engagement and Inner Dialogue with the Cultures and Religions of Melanesia* (Siegburg: Verlag Franz Schmitt, 2014), 32.

away from home). This 'logic of retribution'[8] and loyalty to one's own take precedence over the more abstract relationships of the Western context, e.g. 'honesty' towards one's company or even the church, the government or the party. In Western eyes, this can be seen as 'corruption'. In Melanesian eyes, it is the basis of all ethics: 'good' means what is good for our group, our people.[9] Even more fundamentally, however, this means that the real purpose of economic activity is not profit or enhancing shareholder value, but the strengthening of human relationships: community. With this, the contrast with Western economic thinking becomes clear – and by no means to the disadvantage of the Melanesians.[10]

This traditional scenario has been subverted and destabilised by the advent of the Western monetary and consumer economy. This is abstract and impersonal, designed to maximise private profit and international in extent. Not that Melanesians haven't learnt very quickly to get into this game: money soon became an end in itself and thus a substitute for traditional value. But the possession of money is individual, not communal. Those who come into money in the Western system find themselves beleaguered by *wantoks*, who as always want their share, but people with paying jobs sometimes open secret accounts to which their

---

8   Trompf, Garry, *Payback: The Logic of Retribution in Melanesian Religions* (Cambridge: Cambridge University Press, 1994).

9   On the traditional Melanesian value system and its transformation in the modern context see Mantovani, *The Dema and the Christ*, 29-41. When I asked an Australian accountant in Papua New Guinea why his firm always seemed to have the most modern computers, his reply was: "Computers don't have *wantoks*".

10   May, John D'Arcy, "Economics and Culture in the South Pacific", Lucia A. Reisch, ed., *Ethical-ecological Investment: Towards Global Sustainable Development* (Frankfurt: IKO-Verlag für Interkulturelle Kommunikation, 2001), 117-122; *id.*, "Economics and Culture in the South Pacific: Some Presuppositions of Ethical Investment in Aboriginal and Melanesian Contexts", Project Group Ethical-Ecological Rating Frankfurt-Hohenheim, eds, *Intercultural Comparability of the Ethical Assessment of Enterprises According to Criteria of Cultural, Social and Environmental Responsibility* (München: ökom Verlag, 2000), 70-76.

relatives have no access. "Cash lacks the inherent communitarian aspect of traditional valuables... Relationships were no longer the key value, but cash"; the moral basis of the culture had changed.[11]

When the Papua New Guinea Highlanders realised that in their favourable climate all they needed to do was plant coffee trees in order to make a lot of money, they soon became rich (till the trees were attacked by diseases they did not know how to prevent); when large multinational mining, timber and fishing companies arrived, people all too hastily transferred to them the right to use their land in the mistaken assumption that they had not relinquished the land itself. Over and over again, they tried their luck with small trade stores, without bothering about correct bookkeeping and punctual payment – the customers were their *wantoks*, after all, who would pay their debts sooner or later. Going into politics was seen as the high road to quick riches, and not a few politicians, like some of the local entrepreneurs, found themselves in a position to buy investment properties in northern Australia.

It was this attitude to the Western-style economy that produced the famous cargo cults of Melanesia over a century ago. In a society permeated by magic it is only rational to believe that the goods which flowed towards the whites in an unbroken stream were produced thanks to some ritual, which the whites kept to themselves. The next step was to start experimenting in order to find out what the ritual was. The result was the bizarre activities, from sexual intercourse with virgins in the gardens to the shaking back and forth of cash registers, which were to produce money out of nothing and create wealth.[12]

---

11 Mantovani, *The Dema and the Christ*, 39-40.
12 Trompf, Garry W., *Melanesian Religion* (Cambridge: Cambridge University Press, 1991), discusses these practices in detail.

Today, people are more level headed and in the Southern Highlands, for example, they negotiate tenaciously with mining companies over every tree they cut down, every house they destroy and every river they pollute. However, the companies are powerful and the people's resistance does not in the end prevent the exploitation of their resources and considerable environmental damage. In extreme cases, as in the enormous Ok Tedi mine in the far west of PNG or the Bougainville copper mine on New Britain, the protests of indigenous landowners at the destruction of the landscape and the employment of people from other parts of the country led to protracted violence and civil war.

The Christian churches, by and large, have tried to uphold different values. As there was practically no modern infrastructure in the early decades of the various missions, the churches themselves set up shipping companies such as Lutheran Shipping, airlines such as the Missionary Aviation Fellowship, publishing houses such as Word Publishing, printing works such as *Kristen Pres*, plantations and other commercial undertakings. Schools, hospitals and health services were founded, and in the course of time those who represented the so-called 'mainline' mission churches came together in ecumenical organisations.[13]

In a certain sense, all this amounted to 'development'. But all too often it anticipated what the Germans in New Guinea and the British in Papua, then the Australians in the mandated Territory of Papua and New Guinea and finally the independent state of Papua New Guinea (from 1975) tried to implement: not *misin* (mission, church) but *bisnis* (capitalistic commerce). As more and more raw materials were discovered, starting with gold but soon

---

13   For a more personal perspective on this, see May, John D'Arcy, *Imagining the Ecumenical: A Personal Journey* (Northcote, Vic.: Morning Star, 2016), chapters 9-12; *id.*, "Whatever Happened to the Melanesian Council of Churches? A Study in Ecumenical Organisation", *Melanesian Journal of Theology* 1 (1985), 138-157.

also copper, oil and gas, the new alien economy led to exploitation which inevitably sowed the seeds of corruption. For the weakest peoples, the modern economy, despite its tantalising promises, is a burden rather than a liberation to a better life. This imbalance is now being exacerbated as China offers to fund infrastructure projects for Pacific nations, thereby putting them into debt and, in the process, laying the foundations for future military installations.

Church circles were and remain strongly conservative, and ideological approaches like 'socialism' or 'liberation theology' had little chance of being accepted. There was an urgent need to rethink development, and to a limited extent the churches succeeded in this. An 'ethic of development' was formulated which at least proposed principles such as the primacy of indigenous initiative and environmental protection.[14] Despite this, it is not easy to shake off the legacy of the early missionaries, whose priority was saving souls rather than social ethics. The economy of Papua New Guinea, as is the case elsewhere in Melanesia, is more and more one-sidedly orientated to the interests of large multinational concerns who regard the islands and their seas as nothing more than raw materials for making profit. The *kaukau* (sweet potato) economy of the villagers is scarcely compatible with the coffee economy of the commercial plantations.[15] Money remains a foreign body, which destabilises relationships in family and village, and the resulting void is filled with alcohol and drugs.

This is beginning to manifest itself dramatically, in ways that are not yet fully understood, as intensifications of harmful sorcery

---

14 Siehe May, John D'Arcy, "Towards the Development of Ethics", in: *Catalyst* 17 (1987), 235-251; Fugmann, Gernot, ed., *Ethics and Development in Papua New Guinea* (Goroka: The Melanesian Institute, 1986).
15 Giddings, Lynn, "Social Impact Study of the Yonki Hydro Scheme: Youth Rehabilitation Services Report", Fugmann, ed., *Ethics and Development*, 149-201, 153.

(*sanguma*) and the persecution of witches,[16] which has recently taken on horrific forms such as public burnings and fatal beatings. This is sadly in line with the appalling treatment of women in Papua New Guinea generally, where women are the victims of two thirds of the physical violence perpetrated by men.

The eschatological thrust of Christian faith has had the effect of disturbing and destroying the emphatically this-worldly mentality of tribal societies, which was undoubtedly a factor in the emergence of the cargo cults. Although these have long been prohibited and hardly ever show themselves in public, the 'cargoist mentality' is in the background of all economic and political thinking.[17] Even more radical were changes in the concept of time itself: instead of being directed to the past – one always performed the same rituals to communicate with and appease the spirits of the ancestors – one had to come to terms with the entirely new idea that the future was open and could be shaped by us. By planning and one's own efforts, one could not only change circumstances and attain the goals one set oneself, but there was also an eschatological future brought about by God, towards which the whole world was tending and which would transform everything. This 'eschatological virus' (Theodor Ahrens) has destabilised much of the Melanesian worldview, not least in the way it frames economic activity.

---

16   Schwarz, Nick, *Thinking Critically about Sorcery and Witchcraft: A Handbook for Christians in Papua New Guinea* (Goroka: The Melanesian Institute, 2011, rev. ed. 2013).

17   Strelan, John, *Search for Salvation: Studies in the History and Theology of Cargo Cults* (Adelaide: Lutheran Publishing House, 1977). Strelan was one of the first to study the cargo cults from a theological perspective.

6.2 Spirit and Money in Buddhism

Although we speak about 'Buddhist countries' such as Thailand or Tibet, Buddhism in its many forms permeates the whole of Asia at a deep cultural level, even where, as in Indonesia, it has virtually disappeared from public view. With the exception of the Philippines and the island states evangelised by Christians, Buddhism has a subtle influence on the ethos of the entire region. This makes it important to investigate whether and how Buddhist values have any effect on economic development there. The Buddha himself, as the texts of the Pali canon portray him, took the responsibility of the powerful for economic justice very seriously. More than once, he is said to have advised kings to strive for social equality if they wanted a peaceful reign. The community of monks (*sangha*) itself is supposed to have been based on the 'republican' structure of the clan societies from which 'Prince' Gautama stemmed. Just as Jesus was well informed about the government of the Roman province of Palestine and its tax policies, so the Buddha, as a member of the *Ksatriya* caste of traders and rulers, moved easily in their circles.

The Buddhist teaching (*dhamma*), although it is psychologically and even philosophically extremely sophisticated, is above all a practice. The path to realisation (in both senses!), in the Buddhist analysis of reality as summarised in the Four Noble Truths, is formulated in the Fourth Truth as the Noble Eightfold Path, a graded practice designed to lead to enlightenment. It includes 'right livelihood' (*samma-ajiva*), which prohibits trading in weapons, human beings, meat, alcohol, drugs and poisons of any kind.[18] This analysis begins with the impermanence (*anicca*,

---

18 May, John D'Arcy, "Gibt es eine buddhistische Wirtschaftsethik?", Maria Hungerkamp and Matthias Lutz, eds, *Grenzenüberschreitende Ethik. Festschrift*

'transitoriness') and insubstantiality (*anatta*, 'no self') of all phenomena. Nothing, neither word nor object nor their ultimate constituents (*dhamma* in a different sense), has existence of itself (*svabhava*); one can never say what it is in itself, except in terms of its interrelatedness with everything else. From this is derived the fundamental interdependence of all phenomena in mutual dependency (*paticca-samuppada*, 'dependent co-origination'): they subsist only as relationships, never as substances in their own right.

The assumption that things are real in themselves and can thus fulfil our needs is at the root of the fundamental frustration (*dukkha*, 'unsatisfactoriness', often translated as 'suffering') that characterises human existence. The aim of Buddhist practice is the definitive overcoming and extirpation (*nirodha*) of craving (*tanha*, 'thirst') and the attainment of a state of equanimity (*upekkha*) or absence of desire. The ground is thus prepared for the complete extinction of all traces of the *kamma* (Sanskrit *karma*, the residue of deeds ruled by desire) which leads to rebirth in the flux of becoming (*samsara*). This equates to the definitive passing over into *nibbana* (Sanskrit *nirvana*, 'blowing out the flame' of existence in *samsara*). This radical realism proves to be an excellent diagnostic tool for criticising the throw-away economy of Western consumer societies, which by now has reached global proportions. It certainly questions the foundations of an economy based on the deceptions of advertising and the creation of artificial needs.[19] It implies an ethic which has been characterised as 'knowledge in practice' (*Praxis der Erkenntnis*), offering guidelines for an

---

für Prof. Dr. Johannes Hoffmann anlässlich seines 60. Geburtstages (Frankfurt a.M.: IKO-Verlag für Interkulturelle Kommunikation, 1997), 65-82.

19   Brodbeck, Karl-Heinz, *Buddhistische Wirtschaftsethik. Eine Einführung* (Berlin: edition steinrich, 2002, new rev. ed. 2011), 35-50; see also Sivaraksa, Sulak, *The Wisdom of Sustainability: Buddhist Economics for the 21st Century* (Kihei, Hawaii: Koa Books, 2009).

economy based on justice.[20]

The Buddhist existential analysis can nevertheless appear otherworldly and unrelated to real life. Historically and paradoxically, monastic wealth became a problem, not unlike the situation that developed in Medieval Europe. The reputation of especially accomplished abbots and the contemplative life of their monasteries attracted more and more wealth in the form of donations by the faithful, which tended to be concentrated in immensely wealthy establishments. In the course of history, this led to revolts by the laity and attempts to dispossess such monasteries. Institutional Buddhism had the effect of bringing about massive redistributions of wealth according to the principle of *dana*, generous donations to monasteries (in some cases even to the extent of making over an entire kingdom or its treasury to the monks – *pro forma*, of course) in order to amass good *karma* for the future rebirths of the rulers in question. Central to the Buddhist evaluation of wealth and prosperity is the attitude of non-attachment.

Unlike Christian monasticism, Buddhism does not regard poverty as a virtue or an ideal; here, as always, it steers a middle path between renunciation and indulgence. Traditionally, the primary goal, for monks and laypeople, was the individual attainment of liberation (*mokkha*) from worldly ties, not by the practice of asceticism but by mental training. Yet it was recognised that a society based on these principles would be characterised by justice and compassion, exemplified in the *sangha*, which therefore had the complementary role of legitimising the authority of those who ruled and criticising them when they deviated from the norm.[21]

---

20   Brodbeck, *Buddhistische Wirtschaftsethik*, 51-66.
21   The essays in Sizemore, Russell F., and Donald K. Swearer, eds, *Ethics, Wealth and Salvation: A Study in Buddhist Social Ethics* (Columbia, SC: University of South Carolina Press, 1990) helpfully synthesized in the editors' Introduction,

The Buddhist establishment of a country like Thailand, however, is far from an edifying example of detachment from wealth and power; rather – as Sulak Sivaraksa never tires of complaining – many monks at the higher levels of the Order enjoy their reputation and privileges to the full. Indeed, contemporary Thai society might be described as rampant capitalism, characterised by rent seeking, corruption and environmental destruction.

It was the achievement of Buddhadasa Bhikkhu, as we have seen, to bring the *dhamma* down to the level of today's social reality and to see liberation as a present task rather than a distant goal. His 'dhammic socialism' may seem moralistic and idealistic to Western observers, especially when it is correlated with a 'dictatorial democracy', but Buddhadasa inspired serious social criticism and economic reform, and not just in Asia.[22]

> The consequences of this reappraisal have been many, including an emphasis on the here-and-now rediscovery of the spiritual dimension of everyday life, a bridging of the lay-monastic fracture, greater compatibility with science, greater intellectual rigor, and the reintegration of political and social issues within a Dhammic worldview.[23]

---

illuminate these aspects of Buddhist economic ethics both historically and philosophically.

22   Buddhadasa, *Dhammic Socialism*, ed. by Donald Swearer (Bangkok: Thai Inter-Religious Commission for Development, 1986).

23   Santikaro Bhikkhu, "Buddhadasa Bhikkhu: Life and Society through the Natural Eyes of Voidness", Queen and King, eds, *Engaged Buddhism*, 147-193. Santikaro continues: "for Buddhadasa Bhikkhu there was no ultimate separation between the social and the spiritual. They are two interpenetrating aspects of the one reality (Dhamma) according to the Law of Nature (Dhamma), that is, interdependency" (154-155).

Thailand's so-called 'development monks' were inspired by him to educate young farmers in new agricultural techniques.[24] The proceeds of their farm work are paid into a fund administered for them by the abbot until they are able to acquire a parcel of land and stand on their own feet. These savings are regarded as *dana*, the laity's traditional giving to the monks, which helps these rural people understand and accept the process. Their 'merits' can thus be understood in the usual sense as the reduction of bad *karma*: development becomes Buddhist. This suggests that the ethical practices of the more progressive elements in Thai society may indeed be correlated with Buddhist teaching, the *dhamma* prized above all earthly wealth. For Buddhadasa, "democracy is a moral rather than a political issue", and "he legitimized socialism as an issue and an approach appropriate to Buddhism, Thai culture, and the current situation".[25]

In the hands of critical Buddhists such as Ken Jones or David Loy these teachings prove to be an effective instrument for unmasking the inhumanity of both socialist and capitalist economies.[26] They open up the possibility of mounting a fundamental critique of the taken for granted assumptions on which modern economics is based – growth, competition, choice, consumption, profit. Loy's critique is built around the ineluctability of 'lack', the emptiness at the heart of reality that no intensity of desire or effort can fill, his reinterpretation of *dukkha* and *anatta* with the help of depth psychology and existential

---

24   Phongphit, Seri, *Religion in a Changing Society: Buddhism, Reform and the Role of Monks in Community Development in Thailand* (Hong Kong: Arena Press, 1988); see May, *Transcendence and Violence*, 93-100.

25   Santikaro, "Buddhadasa Bhikkhu", 165, 170.

26   Jones, Ken, *The Social Face of Buddhism: An Approach to Political and Social Activism* (London: Wisdom Publications, 1989); Loy, David, *A Buddhist History of the West: Studies in Lack* (Albany: State University of New York Press, 2002).

philosophy. The modest achievements of critical Buddhists in countries like Thailand and Sri Lanka, which find expression in social movements and practical initiatives but are often overlooked, could be an example of how local initiatives become the building blocks of an ethically responsible global civil society.

6.3 Globalisation and the Plurality of Values

Social inequality is one of the most odious results of economic globalisation.[27] Despite all protestations to the contrary, the amassing of capital does not stimulate the economy but serves to enrich still further the already obscenely wealthy 'one per cent'. Even the International Monetary Fund (IMF) has sounded the alarm, because increasing inequality distorts and destabilises the whole economic system. But the idea that the super-rich should be adequately taxed, and in particular that a transaction tax (Tobin tax) should be levied on massive global financial transfers, is claimed to diminish profits and distort competition.[28]

That multinational concerns should be appropriately taxed in the countries where they make their profits is regarded as politically inopportune by governments who depend on these companies to provide economic infrastructure or even to finance election campaigns. We now know, for example, that Facebook has allowed the personal data of 87 million users to be illegally appropriated in order to manipulate elections in a number of

---

27   One of its sharpest critics is the Nobel Prize winner Joseph Stiglitz, see Stiglitz, Joseph, *Globalization and Its Discontents* (New York: Norton, 2002); *id.*, *The Price of Inequality* (London: Allen Lane, 2012).

28   Schulmeister, Stephan, "Destabilisierende Finanzspekulation und ihre Eindämmung durch eine Transaktionssteuer", Hoffmann, Johannes, and Gerhard Scherhorn, eds, *Eine Politik für Nachhaltigkeit. Neuordnung der Kapital- und Gütermärkte* (Erkelenz: Altius Verlag, 2009), 197-219; Gabriel, Klaus, "Das schnelle Geld. Die Spekulation als solche und ihre ethische Bewertung", *ibid.*, 220-236.

countries.[29] The ideology of neo-liberal – more accurately, neo-conservative – capitalism blinds many to the appalling effects an economy based solely on making money has on the most needy, on nation states and on the global economy itself. The near-collapse of this artificially constructed system, which has less and less connection with the actual economy of production and marketing, in the global financial crisis of 2007-2009, seems to have done nothing to shake these dogmas; on the contrary, the roulette wheel of financial speculation is spinning just as before.[30]

The problem with financial capital is that it has become detached from the 'real capital' of human and natural resources, externalising the costs of destroying the substance from which it lives instead of absorbing them[31] and, as the World Council of Churches said at its Canberra Assembly (1991), 'letting the prices tell the truth'. Concepts such as ecology and sustainability come a distant second to maximising profits and enhancing shareholder value. There have been numerous court judgments prohibiting corporations from reversing these priorities, going back to Henry Ford's attempt, frustrated by the courts, to halve the price of the Model T and raise the wages of his workers by 5 per cent so that they could buy it: a corporation's first responsibility is profitability.[32] This amounts to "ensuring the expansion of

---

29 "Egg on the Facebook: The Silicon Valley leviathan faces the biggest crisis of its short, loud and lucrative existence", *The Age* (Melbourne), 24/3/2018, 28-29.

30 Scherhorn, Gerhard, *Wachstum oder Nachhaltigkeit. Die Ökonomie am Scheideweg* (Erkelenz: Altius Verlag, 2015). A summary of the main theses of this empirically based and ethically profound study may be found in Scherhorn, Gerhard, *Nachhaltige Entwicklung. Die besondere Verantwortung des Finanzkapitals / Sustainable development: The outstanding responsibility of financial capital* (Erkelenz: Altius Verlag, 2008), from which I quote in what follows.

31 Scherhorn, *Sustainable Development*, 120-121: to externalize expenses is to "get rich at the expense of others, the environment, the general public", 121.

32 Scherhorn, *Sustainable Development*, 132.

capitalism by eliminating ethical obstacles".[33] It is no exaggeration to say that current political and economic conditions "*force* them [companies, JDM] to decide *against* a sustainable development".[34] Confirming what we observed about the social economies of Melanesia, Scherhorn remarks:

> [A]s a species, people are dependent upon co-operation and mutual trust; their evolutionary success can only be explained by the fact that people in earlier, smaller societies managed to restrain selfishness by manners and rules of cooperative behaviour… The mental distance between people is heightened already, once money is involved; they are less sure to rely on the help of others and are more reluctant to help others themselves.[35]

That economics as a science and the economic policies based on it have succeeded in obliterating any consideration of the social and ecological consequences of financial capitalism is a relatively recent phenomenon.

Words such as 'faith' and 'dogma' are only partly metaphorical in this context: the world economy is indeed a universal value system based on faith, whose theology is the science of economics and whose ideology is the myth of uninterrupted progress. The Buddhist critic David Loy has called it the first world religion that really deserves the name,[36] and the Catholic mystic Thomas Merton once remarked that the term 'cargo cult' is more appropriate in this context than in Melanesia.

---

33   Scherhorn, *Sustainable Development*, 134.
34   Scherhorn, *Sustainable Development*, 186.
35   Scherhorn, *Sustainable Development*, 180.
36   Loy, *A Buddhist History*, 197-210; see Cox, Harvey, "The Market as God: Living in the New Dispensation", *The Atlantic Monthly*, March 2009, digital edition.

From the very beginnings of human literature in the Sumerian epic of Gilgamesh, who set out to tame the wild forest dweller Enkidu and fortify his city of Uruk on a futile quest for immortality, economic concerns have been entwined with the myths that portray the struggle of good and evil.[37] The Hebrew Bible established the paradigm of a linear history which *progresses* from event to new event rather than perpetually returning to its point of origin, as the Gilgamesh story does, thereby reinforcing the imperative to till the soil, do business and accumulate wealth.[38] There is no stigma attached to this, but it does raise moral issues at every turn: "The entire history of the Jewish nation is interpreted and perceived in terms of morality".[39] Joseph's interpretation of Pharaoh's dream as a cycle of seven fat years succeeded by seven lean years is a precursor of economic planning – in today's terms, the business cycle. Themes such as social justice and community cohesion are insisted upon again and again, with special emphasis on generosity towards the needy and the inclusion of the alien.[40]

These issues also feature prominently in the New Testament, where there are frequent references to economic matters, not least in the parables of Jesus. The central notion of 'redemption' is economic: in the ancient world it meant buying a person's release from slavery. But strictly speaking, freedom, like anything of intrinsic value, has no price: it is a gift, and unlike Melanesian 'payback' it does not invite reciprocity; it cannot be earned.[41] In short, "Christ cancels the economy of good and evil".[42] The

---

37   This is the starting point of Sedlacek's study *Economics of Good and Evil*.
38   Sedlacek, in his chapter on the Old Testament, points to the secularisation of nature and politics in this perspective.
39   Sedlacek, *Economics of Good and Evil*, 62.
40   Sedlacek, *Economics of Good and Evil*, 80.
41   Sedlacek, *Economics of Good and Evil*, 135-137. Similarly, 'sin' in Greek meant debt, 167.
42   Sedlacek, *Economics of Good and Evil*, 148.

awareness that economics involves values that are beyond price carries over into Medieval thinkers such as Thomas Aquinas and on into the work of Adam Smith, the Scottish ethicist who is regarded as the father of modern economics, though his two passing references to the 'invisible hand' of cumulative self-interest have been distorted into a legitimation for neo-liberal moral agnosticism.[43]

There is no point insisting – as politicians and scientists are fond of doing – that religion should remain in the church, temple or mosque and not interfere with the economy. Rather, it is the religions that created and transmitted the ethical values which for innumerable peoples are the foundation of human community, the stability of social structures and the relationship to the natural environment. The task ahead, an 'ecumenical' one in the truest sense of the word, is now to work through the differences and contradictions of the religious traditions in a process of dialogue, to enable the religions to work *together* to help solve humankind's most urgent problems. If Hans Küng's proposal that the religions should contribute to a global ethos or ethic has any practical application, then surely here.[44] This contribution of the religions would consist in making human relationships – not only to God or the transcendent, but to other human beings who might be alien or antagonistic, and to nature – the basis of intensive dialogue and theological reflection. The examples of Melanesian and Buddhist ethics show that there is indeed a basis for such reflection which is not necessarily 'Western', but could be correlated with Christian and Islamic principles. We shall return to this possibility in Part III.

---

43   Sedlacek, *Economics of Good and Evil*, Chapter 7.
44   Küng, Hans, *Projekt Weltethos* (München-Zürich: Piper, 1990); Küng, Hans, und Karl-Josef Kuschel, eds, *Wissenschaft und Weltethos* (München-Zürich: Piper, 1998); *id.*, *A Global Ethic for Global Politics and Economics* (London: SCM, 1997); Küng, Hans, und Karl-Josef Kuschel, eds, *Erklärung zum Weltethos. Die Deklaration des Parlamentes der Weltreligionen* (München-Zürich: Piper, 1993).

Chapter 7: Refugees: Humans Without Rights?

(Indonesia and Australia)

If land, as we have been discussing, is such a fundamental human value, which binds people so closely to the 'place' where they were born and where they feel safe, what could motivate them to leave their native place for ever? Some, like my Irish forebears, do so for economic reasons, to escape irremediable poverty; others do so because their lives are in danger, whether from wars or repression by dictatorial regimes. More recently, a third category has become apparent: ecological refugees, who leave country that has become uninhabitable because of rising sea levels or endless drought. Such a future is an immediate prospect for a number of Pacific islands; on Tuvalu it is already happening.

The distinction between 'political' and 'economic' refugees is problematical: political conditions are often at the root of economic catastrophe or ecological destruction. But for whatever motives, involuntarily forsaking the land to which one owes one's existence, and the people to whom one is bound by love and kinship, is always traumatic. In a globalising world with its terrorist movements, civil wars and environmental catastrophes, however, this is the fate of more than 65 million people worldwide, though many of these are internal refugees who have not fled across international borders.

Millions of refugees stream out of the Maghreb countries, left in ruins by the 'Arab Spring', as well as from Syria, Iraq, Afghanistan and Iran; tens of thousands from Latin America attempt to penetrate the southern border of the USA by any means. Persecuted Tamils are still trying to escape from Sri Lanka. In Africa hundreds of thousands trek from one destabilised country to another until they are funnelled across the Mediterranean into Europe. People who are prepared to cling to the undercarriage of trucks or be shut into containers to reach Western Europe; who cross the Timor Sea or the Mediterranean in rickety boats or unstable inflatables; who attempt to walk through the Channel Tunnel to reach England, must surely be desperate.

This prompts the question: why? How much responsibility does the West bear for the conditions these people are fleeing, from failed states that were often artificially created to further Western economic interests? To what extent are their countries of origin responsible, where inept governments cling to power by instigating civil wars and tolerating terrorist movements? What is the obligation of rich countries to accept such refugees? Globalisation creates and intensifies these problems; all too often the religions make them worse by aligning themselves with nationalism and sectarianism.

These are the complex topics through which we must now find our way. We shall look first at the situation in Indonesia, the transit country for refugees on their way to Australia but with internal refugee problems of its own (7.1). We shall then examine Australia's shameful refugee policies, which are now attracting favourable attention from the EU (7.2). In conclusion, we shall ask how the principles of inalienable human dignity and human rights, which have their roots in religious convictions, can be brought to bear on such situations (7.3).

7.1 Transit and *Transmigrasi* in Indonesia

Indonesia with its 250 million people and 17,000 islands is one of the most densely populated countries on earth, especially on the main island of Java. For this reason, Indonesian governments have maintained a program of *transmigrasi*, moving people from the centres of overpopulation to the least populated parts of the country.[1] One could call these forcibly resettled people internal refugees. The majority are Malay Muslim rice growers. Thousands of them have been transferred to West Papua, where the indigenous population consists mainly of Melanesian Christian hunters and gardeners.

West Papua was originally claimed by the Dutch as they colonised the so-called spice islands. Since the area was regarded as primitive and inaccessible, there was practically no attempt to develop it. In the Second World War, the territory was overrun by the Japanese; when it was reconquered by the Americans, Hollandia (the present capital Jayapura on the north-east coast) served as General Douglas MacArthur's operational base. After the war the situation was fluid: the Dutch wanted 'their' colony back, the Indonesians under the leadership of the hero of independence and first president, Sukarno, held firm to the principle that the borders of former colonies are inviolable.

The new Republic of Indonesia was to extend 'from Meran to Merauke', from the far north-west to the south-east corner. But Melanesian West Papua does not fit easily into Malay and Muslim Indonesia – except for its rich mineral resources. The Americans wanted a quick solution; the Australians, whose aim was to grant independence to the whole of New Guinea – but not prematurely – caved in and opened the way for a referendum orchestrated

---

1 Beyer, Ulrich, *Ein Volk zieht um. Indonesiens staatliches Umsiedlungsprogramm und die Kirchen* (Frankfurt: Lembeck, 1988).

by Indonesia, in which about 1000 tribal leaders intimidated by threats voted to have West Papua incorporated into the Indonesian republic. Even the UN representative called this so-called 'Act of Free Choice' a farce.[2]

Thus began the long drawn-out suffering of the West Papuans, which still continues, barely noticed by the rest of the world, and has driven 10,000 refugees over the border into Papua New Guinea. The whole island of New Guinea is rich in all kinds of resources; the copper mines and gas and oil fields of West Papua are a major source of income for the Indonesian economy. The western half of the island is, therefore, a crucial support for the power of both the military and the government.[3] It follows that there is little prospect that the West Papuans, who are being overtaken in numbers by the Indonesian 'transmigrants', will ever achieve real autonomy, let alone independence. This conclusion is all the more painful in the light of the unexpected liberation of East Timor from Indonesian rule. The province, which used to be called Irian Jaya, has now been divided into 'Papua' and 'West Papua' in order to weaken the Melanesians' attempts to gain autonomy and distract them with the spoils of corruption – jobs, money, status.

We now have to come to terms with the spectacle of those West Papuans who have managed to get a foothold in government and civil service positions neglecting and exploiting their own compatriots. The Indonesian military and government officials look down on the Papuans as 'apes' and 'primitives'; their racism is flaunted openly and often takes the form of repression and even

---

[2] Saltford, John, *The United Nations and the Indonesian Takeover of West Papua, 1962-1969: The Anatomy of Betrayal* (London and New York: Routledge Curzon, 2003).

[3] Leith, Denise, *The Politics of Power: Freeport in Suharto's Indonesia* (Honolulu: University of Hawaii Press, 2003).

shootings carried out with impunity. The mere act of raising the morning star flag, which the West Papuans have made their own, is a crime. It is all the more remarkable that all religious groups are engaged in dialogue with one another and with the government to bring about peace and progress.[4] This emphatically includes better relations with the Muslim immigrants, whether voluntary or compulsory.

Indonesia not only receives refugees from neighbouring Southeast Asian countries, South Asia and the Middle East, it produces them internally through the persecution of Christians and sectarian conflict between Sunni and Shi'ite Muslims. This is relatively new and is particularly tragic, because Indonesian Islam was traditionally strongly influenced by Sufism and was thus more relaxed and tolerant than elsewhere. But the introduction of Wahhabi Islam by Arab traders already in the nineteenth century has caused considerable tension in Indonesian Islam, as we saw above (3.1). This is the context of Indonesia's role in the regional refugee situation, to which we shall return in the next section. There are said to be 14,000 refugees from various countries marooned on the south coast of Java as they wait for the chance to seek asylum in Australia. An example of the pressures generating refugee flows from well beyond Indonesia's shores was the Andaman Sea crisis of 2014.

Similar to Sri Lanka, where Singhalese Buddhist nationalism caused mainly Hindu Tamils to flee, in Myanmar (Burma)

---

4   Tebay, Neles, *Interfaith Endeavours for Peace in West Papua* (Aachen: Missio, 2006); May, John D'Arcy, "Jakarta and Jayapura: The Dialogue of Religions and 'Papua, Land of Peace'", Carole M. Cusack and Christopher Hartney, eds, *Religion and Retributive Logic: Essays in Honour of Professor Garry W. Trompf* (Leiden and Boston: Brill, 2010), 19-42; Mawene, M.T., "Christ and Theology of Liberation in West Papua", *Exchange* 33 (2004), 153-179; Ireeuw, T.M., "An Appeal for Melanesian Christian Solidarity", Garry W. Trompf, ed., *The Gospel is Not Western: Black Theologies from the Southwest Pacific* (Maryknoll: Orbis Books, 1987), 170-182.

infuriated Buddhists, egged on by nationalistic monks, have been persecuting the Muslim Rohingyas of Rakhine State on the border with Bangladesh. The situation is much more complicated than a mere sectarian conflict. Rohingyas have lived in this area for centuries, but have never been recognised by the Burmese or granted citizenship with corresponding civil rights. The brutality of this deliberate campaign by the Myanmar military is shocking: since the atrocities were sparked by the attack of a Rohingya militant group on a police post on 25 August 2017, 354 villages have been partially or completely destroyed, resulting in 835,000 Rohingya seeking refuge across the border in Bangladesh. Arson, rape and infanticide have continued despite international attempts at mediation. A hastily brokered repatriation agreement was described under these circumstances as a "public relations stunt". This was the climax of a process of what the UN called "textbook ethnic cleansing" that had been going on for some time.[5] In 2014, some 54,000 people took to boats on the Bay of Bengal and the Andaman Sea. Mostly from Bangladesh and Myanmar, these desperate refugees were trying to reach Thailand, Malaysia or Indonesia.

> There was considerable suffering both during and at the end of the trip. The UNHCR estimated that 540 people died in 2014 during these journeys, due to starvation, dehydration and beatings by crew members – many bodies were simply thrown overboard. At the end of the trip, many survivors told of being held in smugglers' camps and made to call relatives to pay for their release. If payment was not immediate, they were beaten or faced serious

---

5   Murdoch, Lindsay, "'Hundreds' of Rohingya villages destroyed", *The Age*, 19 December 2017; "Devastation must be seen to be understood", *The Age*, 27 December 2017.

mistreatment. Hundreds of people may have died in the camps from illness, starvation, dehydration and killings by smugglers when they tried to escape or could not pay... More boats left in the early months of 2015, with a further 25,000 people fleeing Myanmar and Bangladesh. By the start of May, a further 370 had died.[6]

On 1 May 2015, the crisis came to a head when a mass grave of more than 50 bodies was discovered in the Sadao district of southern Thailand. There were arrests and reprimands, and Thai, Malaysian and Indonesian authorities began intercepting asylum seeker boats and pushing them back out to sea. "By 12 May between 6,000 and 8,000 people were stranded on the boats, many without food or water. However, amid the chaos of ongoing boat pushbacks, Indonesian and Malaysian local officials and fishermen rescued around 3,000 people. Others stranded swam to shore from their boats".[7]

The immediate crisis was eventually resolved, though "more than 1,100 – both Myanmar Muslims from Rakhine State and Bangladeshis – remained in shelters and Immigration Detention Centres in Indonesia, Thailand and Malaysia". Asked whether any of the refugees would be resettled in Australia, then prime minister Tony Abbot infamously replied: "Nope, nope, nope".[8] This brief account of the regional situation serves to put Australia's asylum seeker policy in context. It is, of course, much more than a matter of religious antagonisms: a number of countries have interests in Myanmar – China because of its natural resources, Pakistan for fear of receiving refugees from Bangladesh, Saudi Arabia in the

---

6   Ward, Tony, *Bridging Troubled Waters: Australia and Asylum Seekers* (North Melbourne: Australian Scholarly Publishing, 2017), 161.
7   Ward, *Bridging Troubled Waters*, 161-162.
8   Ward, *Bridging Troubled Waters*, 162-163.

hope of making converts to Wahhabism. Yet the fact remains that Buddhist Burmese are targeting Muslim Rohingyas *because they are Muslims*. International attention is focused on Aung San Suu Kyi as the *de facto* leader of Myanmar and a Buddhist champion of human rights, because she is unwilling to acknowledge the atrocities or even to use the term Rohingya, though the difficulties of her situation are not always appreciated: she has no real power vis-à-vis the military, she knows there is little sympathy among her supporters for 'Bangladeshi foreigners', and she needs to foster a climate of democratic freedom in her own country. Nonetheless, real leadership on the part of any of the religions involved is sadly lacking.

7.2 Australia: The Great Refusal

In the eyes of the Aborigines, the only humans who have inhabited *ab origine* what became the Australian continent, the Portuguese, Dutch, French and British who arrived in the course of the seventeenth and eighteenth centuries were all 'boat people'. Ironically, in the light of recent developments, the continent was originally intended as a penal colony so harsh and cruel that it would deter criminals in Britain and rebels in Ireland. But once the convicts acquired land of their own and became successful entrepreneurs, the prospect of going there became extremely attractive to those at home with ambitions to turn wilderness into farm land and make their fortune. The tragedy, as we have seen (5.1), is that none of these Europeans had the faintest inkling of the antiquity and sophistication of the cultures that had enabled the Aborigines to survive in this unforgiving country for millennia. A further irony is that it is precisely successive waves of immigrants from many different parts of the world that have made Australia the successful multicultural society it is.

Where, then, did things go wrong? There were sporadic but deliberate attempts by some settlers in various locations to kill off Aboriginal inhabitants who resisted dispossession of their land by Europeans. There was the enslavement of Pacific Islanders to work as 'Kanaks' on the sugar plantations, known as 'blackbirding'. There were a number of anti-Chinese riots on the goldfields, notably at Lambing Flat, as the Chinese competed with other miners, which eventually led to restrictions on the numbers of Chinese allowed to disembark in Australia.

Australia allowed British Jews to emigrate, but not non-British, for most of the early twentieth century. The famous 'Dunera boys' were not all Jewish nor technically refugees; they were expelled from Britain as 'enemy aliens' on the *Dunera* and interned in detention centres on arrival in Australia in 1940. In late 1938, the government offered to take 15,000 Jewish refugees fleeing the Nazis. By the outbreak of war, only 7,000 had arrived. The Archbishop of Melbourne, Daniel Mannix, was one of those who were outspoken on the duty to receive these refugees.[9]

All this casts a shadow over Australia's treatment of foreigners and helps to explain the emergence and continuance of the infamous White Australia policy, enshrined in the constitution at federation and not formally abrogated till the Whitlam Labor government ended Australia's participation in the Vietnam war. The conservative prime minister Malcolm Fraser agreed to accept some 56,000 refugees from Vietnam, among them over 2000 'boat people', between 1976 and 1981. They would otherwise have ended up in communist 're-education camps' or been robbed, raped or murdered by pirates in the South China Sea.

---

9   Once again I wish to thank Dr Bruce Duncan for helpful advice on the presentation of these historical data.

Around this time, some 200,000 Asians have settled in Australia and become loyal and industrious citizens, among them Hieu Van Le, born in 1954 in Quang Tri, South Vietnam, who fled with his wife and forty others on a boat which reached Darwin. After a notable career as an accountant and many honours, on 14 September 2014 he became governor of South Australia, the first Asian to hold such a vice-regal position. Another, Vincent Long Van Nguyen OFM Conv., born in Vietnam in 1961, arrived on a boat with his parents and was made Bishop of Parramatta on 5 May 2016. Many other Asian refugees and their children have had success as business people, artists, scientists, doctors and writers.

I was in Germany in October and November 2015 when the human tsunami of refugees fleeing the wars in Syria and elsewhere in the Middle East reached Europe, sweeping aside border controls and EU treaties and flowing through the Balkans to Italy and Greece and on via Austria into Germany, where a million had to be accommodated in that year alone. Like water flowing around obstacles, they kept coming till European governments began intercepting boats in the Mediterranean and the Aegean, reaching agreements with transit countries, especially Turkey, and closing their borders. The legacy of this period is the rise of populist anti-immigration – and often anti-Muslim – parties in most European countries, notably in areas like Eastern Germany, Hungary, Poland and the Czech Republic with little experience of foreign immigration. Compared with this crisis, the numbers trying to reach Australia are tiny, especially when one remembers that those who arrive by air and overstay their visas far outnumber those who come by boat.

> 407,000 people came to Australia over the last twenty years either as refugees or seeking asylum. More than half (53%) came as part of the Humanitarian

program, arriving in Australia after being assessed as refugees overseas. Another third sought asylum after arriving by air, but were little noticed. Boat arrivals totalled 60,000 over these 20 years – only 14% of the total, and fewer than half the number of air arrivals... some 90% of boat arrivals were successful with their asylum claims, while fewer than half of air arrivals were successful.[10]

Nevertheless, the fact that between 1998 and 2002 and again between 2009 and 2013 thousands began crossing the Timor Sea without visas in unseaworthy vessels provided by people smugglers touched a deep nerve in the Australian psyche with its repressed memories of the 'yellow peril' of invasion from Asia. The trauma was exacerbated when hundreds drowned in the attempt.

The 1951 *Convention Relating to the Status of Refugees* defines a refugee as one who

> owing to a well-founded fear of being persecuted for reasons of race, religion, nationality, membership of a particular social group or political opinion, is outside the country of his nationality and... as a result of such events, is unable or, owing to such fears, is unwilling to return to it.[11]

This principle was obscured by the constant repetition of labels such as 'illegal immigrants' or 'unauthorised maritime arrivals', as if people fleeing in fear of their lives would be able to get the correct stamps in their passports or could wait to be processed by the UN refugee agency (the oft-cited, but non-existent 'queue'). Of course, desperate people use desperate means, and

---

10   Ward, *Bridging Troubled Waters*, 2.
11   Cited by Ward, *Bridging Troubled Waters*, 13.

many subterfuges were employed, such as destroying documents before arriving in Australia or leaving family members behind in the belief that they could be brought to Australia subsequently.

For those whose applications were successful, the Howard government introduced Temporary Protection Visas (TPVs) in October 1999, of which some 11,000 were issued between 1999 and 2007. The boats kept coming, and things came to a head when in August 2001 433 asylum seekers on a sinking boat were taken aboard the Norwegian freighter *Tampa*, which was refused entry to Australian waters. They were transferred by the navy to Nauru, and legislation was passed which excised the islands asylum seekers most often tried to reach from the Australian migration zone, thus making it impossible to apply for asylum there.

In September 2001, offshore processing centres were opened on Nauru in the South Pacific and Manus Island in Papua New Guinea, where asylum seekers were kept in atrocious conditions while their claims were being examined, a process that could and did take years. Even though the vast majority were recognised as refugees, they were told that they would never be allowed to settle in Australia. These steps, and the infamous insinuation by Howard in October 2001 that asylum seekers were throwing their children overboard in order to force the navy to rescue them, won him re-election with the slogan 'We will decide who comes to this country and the circumstances in which they come'.[12]

An extraordinary succession of governments and prime ministers complicated the issue further, but for all of them a hard line on border protection was a given because it was a vote winner. In its desperation to find somewhere other than Australia to send asylum seekers, in July 2010 the Labor government even approached the tiny, newly-independent nation of East Timor,

---

12   Ward, *Bridging Troubled Waters*, 58-59.

and an attempt to do a refugee swap with Malaysia was frustrated by the High Court on 11 August 2011. In 2012, Australia agreed with Nauru (14 September) and Papua New Guinea (21 November) to re-open offshore processing centres there. Kevin Rudd's action in closing the centres and resettling the refugees in Australia was accompanied by a dramatic increase in boat arrivals, and in an effort to salvage Labor's vote at the 2013 election, he not only re-opened the centres but declared that refugees arriving by boat would never be permanently settled in Australia, a principle gratefully upheld by subsequent Coalition governments to this day. Tony Abbott's 'stop the boats' rhetoric nevertheless won him the election and from then on Australia's asylum seeker policies have become ever more militarised and inhumane, turning boats back to Indonesia and incarcerating some 2,000 refugees on Nauru and Manus indefinitely.

Violations of the most basic human rights, such as health treatment for the seriously ill and suicide prevention, were routine. Seriously ill detainees were grudgingly and quietly admitted to Australia for urgent medical attention only after court battles. It took a defeat on the floor of parliament in February 2019 for the coalition government to concede that those requiring treatment could be evacuated to Australia, but only to the reopened detention centre on Christmas Island with its six-bed clinic and minimal facilities. Staff of the service agencies administrating the centres who divulged to the media what conditions were really like were threatened with two years' jail. Asylum seekers from Sri Lanka were confined aboard an Australian warship for a month while their applications were cursorily reviewed before being brought back to Colombo, and in June 2015 Australian border personnel paid Indonesian sailors thousands of dollars to return refugees to Indonesia. New Zealand's offer to take 150 of these each year was rejected on the grounds that it would open a 'back door' to Australia, and in September 2014 Cambodia – one of the most corrupt and authoritarian countries in Southeast Asia – was prevailed upon to accept seven refugees, at a total cost of some $44.8 million.

Nothing illustrates better the absurdity of the whole policy, except perhaps the bland assertion that the Manus Island detainees, once the High Court of Papua New Guinea ordered the centre to be closed, could be resettled in that country, in which anyone without kinship ties and some claim on land is a *rabisman*, a person of no status whatsoever. The islands themselves now become detention centres, which the refugees are forbidden to leave. On Manus as on Nauru, the refugees have been treated abominably by the local population, who understandably have no place for the foreigners of alien culture and religion foisted upon them by opportunistic governments.[13] Their plight has been vividly described the Iranian Kurd Behrouz Boochani in his 2018 book – written in secret on a mobile phone – *No Friend But the Mountains*. The treatment of refugees will draw alongside the Stolen Generations as one of the darkest chapters in Australian history.

Though some progress has been made with Indonesia to thwart the people smugglers and President Trump has reluctantly agreed to abide by the 'dumb deal' made with his predecessor to accept some of the refugees after 'extraordinary vetting', as a result of which the last children have left Nauru, the whole episode is an appalling tragedy. One thing glaringly missing in the saga is regional co-operation to achieve a humane approach to the problem with Asia-Pacific neighbours. Another is a serious attempt to address the tragic situations of poverty and oppression in the countries

---

13   For a fuller account of these complicated manoeuvres see Ward, *Bridging Troubled Waters*, Chapter 4 and 76-83.

from which the refugees come. At America's behest, Australia has willingly involved itself in the wars they are fleeing; other Western countries have supplied arms to various parties to these conflicts; and the instability that generates the violence is in many cases the product of Western colonial policies in the past.

Robert Manne calls the key political developments we have sketched above 'Howard's curse' – manipulating the treatment of asylum seekers to win votes – and 'Rudd's curse' – the determination not to settle boat people in Australia. They have resulted in the absolutism that bedevils the asylum policies of both major parties and the 'automaticity' (Vaclav Havel) of an out of touch bureaucracy and political class that have lost the capacity to appreciate the horror being inflicted upon these people.[14] In view of the pressure of refugee numbers and the readiness of people smugglers to mobilise at the first sign of an opening, it is axiomatic that the integrity of borders must be preserved, though more transparently than is the case under Operation Sovereign Borders.

This has now been assured: since 2013, 32 vessels carrying 800 persons have been intercepted, and diplomatic arrangements with Indonesia are in place, though much more must be done to ensure adequate offshore processing of applications so that refugees are not left languishing for years in transit camps. The only thing that now stands in the way of resettling in Australia the 655 people left after the camps have been closed and some of those detained for up to five years (939 on Nauru and 716 on Manus) have been accepted by third countries is the threat of electoral annihilation for any party seen as 'soft' on borders and refugees.[15]

---

14 Manne, Robert, "How the fortress came to pass", *The Age* (Melbourne), 4/3/2018), an excerpt of the essay "How We Came to Be So Cruel" in his book *On Borrowed Time* (Melbourne: Black Inc, 2018).

15 Brennan, Frank, "Close the camps now and stop the posturing", *Eureka Street* 28/10 (2018). Brennan does not explicitly advocate resettlement in Australia.

Many Australians, not least in the churches, are deeply ashamed of these cruel policies, which are ostensibly designed to 'send a message' to people smugglers and deter asylum seekers, but also serve to bolster the election prospects of the main political parties. Under the leadership of Bishop Vincent Long Van Nguyen, himself a boat person from Vietnam, the Australian Bishops Conference in its 2015-2016 Social Justice Statement emphatically condemned the current policy.[16] In the course of the twentieth century, the bishops have played a significant part in immigration debates. They supported post-war immigration and assisted the integration of 'New Australians' in church and society through their social and pastoral organisations. They too had to overcome the prevailing mentality of 'assimilation', conformity with supposedly normative Australian values and ways of life. But in their official statements they acknowledged cultural pluralism. The Catholic Church condemned the White Australia policy in the past and argued for properly regulated immigration, and now, together with other churches, it advocates the acceptance of refugees.[17] Some Anglicans have even advocated opening their churches as places of refuge for asylum seekers in the ancient tradition of *sanctuarium*.[18] The Australian Council of Churches

---

[16] Australian Catholic Bishops Conference, *For Those Who've Come Across the Seas: Justice for Refugees and Asylum Seekers*, Social Justice Statement 2015-16. The document estimates that there are 3.8 million refugees in the Asia-Pacific region. In 2014, 53,000 people attempted the dangerous sea crossing through the Bay of Bengal to Thailand, Malaysia and Indonesia.

[17] Madigan, Patricia, "Graced by Migration: An Australian Perspective", in Elaine Padilla und Peter Phan, ed., *Christianities in Migration: The Global Perspective* (New York: Palgrave Macmillan, 2016), 135-152. The title of this extremely helpful overview of the whole immigration debate refers to one of the Bishops Conference's most important documents, *Graced by Migration: Implementing a National Vision in Pastoral Care for a Multicultural Australian Church* (2007).

[18] Williamson, Raymond K., *Pilgrims of Hope: An Ecumenical Journey 1980-2010* (Northcote, Vic.: Morning Star, 2014), Chapter 10, which documents the initiatives of Australian churches in immigration and refugee policy.

has taken numerous initiatives in accepting refugees and aiding their social integration.

7.3 Compassion and Action

Buddhist, Christian and Muslim ethical values converge in the concept of compassion (*karuna, agape, hadiyya*). Johann Baptist Metz has even suggested that 'compassion' should be Christianity's 'world program' today.[19] The virtues of sympathy and empathy – the ability to 'suffer with' others and 'suffer in' their inmost feelings, which is central to the philosophy of Emmanuel Levinas – could form a bridge to the values of other religions. In the light of this, Metz's proposal deserves consideration. He suggests that empathy and compassion in themselves are not 'political' enough to support a viable social ethic and that Buddhism is weak in these areas,[20] but we have seen that the opposite is the case. The elemental human attitude of sharing intuitively the sufferings of others figures again and again in debates about the treatment of refugees, despite the efforts of politicians to disparage such 'soft' reactions. The words and actions of Pope Francis and the German Chancellor Angela Merkel bear witness to our responsibility to alleviate suffering, which transcends political tactics and national interests. As the 2015 refugee crisis unfolded, Merkel reminded her critics that her party is the *Christian* Democratic Union.

The question remains how Buddhists in Myanmar, Muslims in Indonesia and Christians in Australia can trample the ethical

---

19   Metz, Johann Baptist, "Compassion. Zu einem Weltprogramm des Christentums im Zeitalter des Pluralismus der Religionen und Kulturen", in: *id. et al.*, eds, *Compassion. Weltprogramm des Christentums. Soziale Verantwortung lernen* (Freiburg-Basel-Wien: Herder, 2000), 9-18; May, John D'Arcy, *Buddhologie und Christologie. Unterwegs zu einer kollaborativen Theologie* (Innsbruck-Wien: Tyrolia Verlag, 2014), Chapter 4.

20   Metz, *Compassion*, 13.

value of compassion underfoot in their pursuit of those who are culturally foreign and religiously alien. Each tradition provides ethical guidelines which should make it possible to find humane solutions to what are undeniably serious problems. The fate of unwanted and rejected immigrants is a well-known global phenomenon; the ethical values that could inspire practical solutions have the potential to form part of global awareness, if only the religions advocated and exemplified them. Shared ethical foundations are not the last word in relations between the religions, but they may well be the first word that sets the scene for dialogue.[21] In global civil society there is room for a pluralism of values; indeed, this should be the normal situation, the framework in which the most fundamental debates take place. Pressing issues such as the treatment of refugees and gender equality have as their context the two most fundamental problems facing us: the erosion of democracy and environmental destruction. In Part III, we turn our attention to the contribution the religions could make to solving these problems.

---

21   May, John D'Arcy, *After Pluralism: Towards an Interreligious Ethic* (Münster-Hamburg-London: LIT Verlag, 2000).

PART III

The Globalisation of Theology: Relativising the Religions?

Chapter 8: Collaborative Theologies?

The prospect of a global civil society opens up the possibility that the religions might do what Christians call 'theology' not against, but with one another. If such theological cooperation is to become a reality, however, the religions must draw closer to one another, and this is still a long way off. The discipline once known as 'comparative religion' is now out of fashion, not least because it tended to employ Western philosophical categories with a Christian background in order to abstract supposedly common factors from the religions. But more recently, 'comparative theology' has detached itself from this historical context and is becoming a discipline in its own right.[1] Our first task will be to give an outline and an estimate of this promising new field (8.1).

In the light of the problems we have encountered in Part II, however, we shall try to go beyond merely comparing different ways of doing theology. We shall ask whether and how it is possible for Christians, despite drastic differences and historical resentments, to identify and work through theological problems together with Buddhists, Muslims and representatives of indigenous traditions. This presupposes that we can clarify what we mean by 'theology' in the first place – no easy task (8.2). Only then can we form a judgment about the possibility of finding a way to create a truly global theology in which the foremost thinkers of all religious traditions could participate (8.3).

---

1   Clooney, Francis X., "The Emerging Field of Comparative Theology: A Bibliographical Review (1889-1995)", *Theological Studies* 56 (1995), 521-550; *id.*, "Comparative Theology", *The Oxford Handbook of Systematic Theology* (Oxford: Oxford University Press, 2007), 653-669; *id.*, *Komparative Theologie. Eingehendes Lernen über religiöse Grenzen hinweg* (Paderborn *et al.*: Schöningh, 2013); Fredericks, James, *Buddhists and Christians: Through Comparative Theology to Solidarity* (Maryknoll: Orbis Books, 2004).

The methodological questions thrown up by such a project are immense. As we have already seen more than once, in the Asia-Pacific context alone, relations between the religions are made difficult by rivalries and animosities, although there are, of course, many promising attempts to reach understanding and cooperation. But these cannot mature unless there is fundamental agreement about reconciling the beliefs of others with one's own to the extent that one can find a common language for theological reflection and the problems it is meant to address.

8.1 Comparative Theology

Comparison is an integral part of all knowing. On encountering what is new, alien and unfamiliar – whether foreign countries, people, cultures, moral standards or views of the world – the first step in coming to terms with the novel is to compare it with what is familiar: 'They do *this* just like us, but they do *that* quite differently…'. The encounter of religions is not dissimilar: the coming together of humanity through immigration, travel, trade and media of communication has raised awareness about the existence of many different religions stemming from very different cultures. But are they *completely* different? To the extent that they can be identified as religions at all, they obviously have something that we (Christians, or others as may be the case) can recognise as common to both of us: Buddhists meditate, Muslims pray, Hindus perform rituals, indigenous peoples celebrate the stages of life and life itself. Already, we find ourselves *comparing* the practices and beliefs of others with our own, if only to recognise the differences better.

Recently, this process of comparative understanding or understanding by comparison has begun to take hold in Christian theology. The great extension of Western influence through mission and colonialism in the nineteenth century not only gave rise to comparative religion, but to the realisation that members of other religious communities reflect on their beliefs in ways that seem comparable to Christian theology. This means that, quite apart from particular religious beliefs and practices, there must be some basis for mutual understanding, namely reason.[2] But reasoning about differences with the scientific attitude of observation and comparison is not yet theology. Clooney approaches this with great caution. The whole point of comparative theology, after all, is to go beyond the imposition of one's own criteria in order to make sense of other religions. Carefully reading the texts of the unfamiliar tradition alongside seemingly similar texts from one's own, one feels one's way step by step into the core content of each faith. Provisionally retaining one's own religious convictions, one learns from the inside, as it were, what really constitutes the alien faith.

Does this imply an explicit methodology? To the extent that one identifies themes in the texts being compared and sets about finding ways of relating them, perhaps; but I am wary of reducing the process to a set of rules. I am therefore very sympathetic to comparative theology's respect for the poetic integrity of texts, its determination to grapple with the 'messy particulars' of interpretation, its readiness to postpone theorising until the often intractable textual material has been patiently worked through. "Comparative Theology is what Comparative Theology Does"[3] seems a good enough approach to method for the time being.

---

[2] Hence the title of Clooney, Francis, *Hindu God, Christian God: How Reason Helps Break Down the Boundaries between Religions* (Oxford: Oxford University Press, 2001).

[3] This is the heading of Part 2 Clooney, Francis, and Klaus von Stosch, *How To Do Comparative Theology: Multiple Paths through Today's Field.* (New York: Fordham University Press, 2017)

Nevertheless, the study of religions confronts us with fundamental questions of meaning, truth and practice, which become all the more acute when juxtaposed through comparison. In a recent article, Paul Knitter picked up a phrase used by John Thatamanil: "Comparative theology done well is a dangerous discipline precisely because it raises provocative questions and threatens to put an end to *business-as-usual* theology".[4] Knitter continues: "I fear that some comparative theologians are not taking their job seriously enough – or they are not following through with what they say they want to do".[5] He goes on to quote a comment he had made previously:

> More pointedly, comparative theology, so far, has been more comparison than theology. There have been intricate comparisons of Christian texts with Hindu texts and of Christian theologians/mystics with Buddhist scholars/mystics. Striking similarities and stark differences have been noted and examined, sometimes meticulously. But, where are the clear, creative, courageous conclusions as to what Christians can learn from these comparisons? What might need to be clarified or changed or discarded in traditional Christian doctrine? Especially on the neuralgic and politically dangerous (for Catholics) issue of the uniqueness of Christ, I am not aware of any comparativists who have learned anything new.[6]

---

[4] Paul F. Knitter, "Comparative Theology Is Not 'Business-as-Usual Theology': Personal Witness from a Buddhist Christian", *Buddhist-Christian Studies* 35 (2015), 181-192, 181 (my emphasis).

[5] Knitter, "Comparative Theology", 181.

[6] Knitter, "Comparative Theology", 182. Knitter then outlines a Buddhist-Christian theology based on the comparative experience of Buddhism's impact on Christian doctrine and Christianity's ethical corrective to Buddhism.

Collaborative Theologies?

This throws down the gauntlet to those who are reluctant to make explicit the questions raised by comparison for Christian 'faith and morals', with particular mention of Francis Clooney and James Fredericks. So with due deference to the comparativists' reluctance to indulge in premature generalisation and too hasty theorising, we need to take up the implications of comparative theology for *everyone's* theology, ours and our Others'.

'Comparative theology', as a term, is not new, but as so often happens it was re-introduced as the title of a genuinely new movement in Christian theology, even though its antecedents go back at least to 1700, and many of us realise it designates more or less what we have been doing for years. The first person to coin the term 'comparative theology' was James Garden (1645-1726) in his 1700 volume *Comparative Theology; or, The True and Solid Grounds of Pure and Peaceable Theology: a subject very necessary, tho' hitherto almost wholly neglected.* The paper contributed by the eminent Dutch scholar Cornelius Petrus Tiele (1830-1902) to the 1893 World's Parliament of Religions in Chicago was entitled "On the Study of Comparative Theology".[7] In today's terminology, these would be roughly equivalent to ecumenical theology – correlating Catholic and Protestant doctrines – and comparative religion – taking an 'objective' view of non-Christian religions in relation to Christianity. It is often rightly said, not least by Frank Clooney, that comparative theology is different by definition from

---

7   See Francis Clooney, *Comparative Theology: Deep Learning Across Religions Borders* (Chichester: Wiley-Blackwell, 2010), 24-35; *id.*, *Komparative Theologie*, Chapter 2; Hintersteiner, Norbert, "Intercultural and Interreligious (Un) Translatability and the Comparative Theology Project", *id.*, ed., *Naming and Thinking God in Europe Today: Theology in Global Dialogue* (Amsterdam and New York: Editions Rodopi, 2007), 465-491, 465. I draw here on a contribution by Anita Ray to the working group on comparative theology at Australian Catholic University.

traditional comparative religion, which nevertheless also used the term.[8]

These early usages were, however, deeply problematic, as the example of J. A. McCulloch makes clear.[9] Remarking wryly that there are no "tribes of atheists", McCulloch asserts that the human is "by nature a religious being" and that the pinnacle of this religiosity is Christianity, which is "absolute and final".[10] Answering his own question, "Is there a comparative method possible in Christian theology?", he acknowledges "some seed of truth" in other religions, especially Judaism, which serves as a *praeparatio evangelica,* for "the human heart was already by nature Christian".[11]

It took the Catholic Church until 1965, in the Declaration on the Relationship of the Church to Non-Christian Religions of Vatican II, *Nostra Aetate*, to reach these conclusions, but it is immediately evident that they can hardly serve as "The Method of Comparative Theology", as McCulloch's opening chapter is entitled. Indeed, the later Vatican document *Dominus Iesus* (2000) showed that the implications of *Nostra Aetate*, especially Art. 4 on relations with the Jews as the first fundamental step towards inter-religious openness, had still not been fully realised.[12] We are thus left with two options: either to develop a 'theology of religions' which overcomes this taken for granted superiority of Christianity, or to withdraw into the business of comparison from some higher plane without making judgments of truth (as traditional comparative religion typically did, concealing

---

8   See Sharpe, Eric, *Comparative Religion: A History* (London: Duckworth, 1975).
9   McCulloch, J.A., *Comparative Theology* (London: Methuen, 1902).
10 McCulloch, *Comparative Theology*, 2.
11 McCulloch, *Comparative Theology*, 3-4.
12 See Pawlikowski, John, "Vatican II's Theological About-face on the Jews: Not yet fully recognized", *The Ecumenist* 37 (2000), 4-6.

its Western Christian philosophical presuppositions while proclaiming its 'neutrality'). Merely noting one's adherence to one's own tradition without developing its implications further does not address the problem of comparison. As the ongoing debate between pluralist theologians like Perry Schmidt Leukel and comparative theologians like Klaus von Stosch makes clear, none of these options is entirely satisfactory.[13]

If comparison with what we know is the first step towards understanding, the second step would be communication: 'Here is my take on why you do it the way you do; have I got it right?' It has long been my conviction that interreligious communication is the basis of all mutual understanding in matters of religion, preferably face to face, but also conceivably by 'scriptural reasoning', being guided by our interlocutors in our interpretation of their texts, rituals, art and so on, and returning the favour to them. A third stage might then be actual collaboration, helping one another to formulate 'theology', doctrinal and practical understanding, *together*. The progress from comparison through communication to collaboration is, of course, an ultimate goal and a profound methodological challenge; but in the situation of mutual alienation and recrimination in which the religions find themselves, it cannot be postponed indefinitely.

This suggests that comparative theology is right to cleave to the 'messy particulars' of inter- and intra-textual work, but also that in this textually mediated conversation generalisations will be arrived at which give expression to the 'deep textures', the symbolic, mythological and conceptual deep structures which generate the texts in the first place. For some, Jungian depth psychology gives

---

13   See Schmidt-Leukel, Perry, "Limits and Prospects of Comparative Theology", and Klaus von Stosch, "Comparative Theology as an Alternative to the Theology of Religions", in Hintersteiner, ed., *Naming and Thinking God*, 493-505, 507-512. I was present for this particular spirited exchange.

access to this often subconscious level of spiritual activity;[14] for others, acknowledgement of the depth dimension of religious experience opens up the possibility of exploring oral traditions such as those of Aboriginal Australia and re-examining doctrinal belief systems in the light of this comparison.[15] Such comparison is a matter of striking a balance between the universal and the particular, *a priori* and *a posteriori*, deductive and inductive – one of the most ancient philosophical figures of thought.

Presupposing the possibility of mastering foreign languages and visiting places of worship in distant lands, Clooney's strategy is promising. Although it is Christian in inspiration, it has universal relevance, because in a time when most societies are multi-religious, their religious communities can scarcely avoid comparing themselves with others and entering into conversation with them. The key point is whether this in every case and in the same sense amounts to 'theology'. This is, after all, a Christian concept. Buddhists have only recently begun talking about 'Buddhist theology' or 'Buddhology'; Jews are generally suspicious of the term (and find 'Christology' completely unacceptable); for Muslims, it tends to take place in the medium of legal reasoning (and 'Trinity' is regarded as *shirk*, polytheistic blasphemy). In the indigenous traditions such as those of the Asia-Pacific, it would have to be entirely reconceived. Theological traditions are not simply abstract theories: rather, they are community orientated, embedded in the social contexts of Church, *sangha*, *ummah*, clan. Nevertheless, the breakthrough to a responsible comparative theology is an important step forward in the reciprocal relations

---

14 See David Tacey, *Beyond Literal Belief: Religion as Metaphor* (Melbourne: John Garratt Publishing, 2015).

15 See Eugene Stockton, *The Deep Within: Towards an Archetypal Theology* (Lawson: Blue Mountains Education and Research Trust, 2011).

of the religions, which finds an appropriate context in global civil society.

The Archimedean point for establishing a theology of religious pluralism has not yet been discovered. In my view, this can only be a collaborative enterprise in full awareness of the secular and religious dimensions of globalisation. But in the meantime it would seem to be irresponsible to defer indefinitely the effort to formulate a hypothesis that would allow the religions to retain their time-honoured identities while breaking out of their 'my religion is better than your religion' isolation and co-operating on the project of establishing genuine peace. Comparative theology's indispensable contribution to this project is the gradual and patient accumulation of a wealth of reciprocal interpretation based on the careful and respectful reading of texts. This goes well beyond the purportedly neutral information supplied by comparative religion but shies away from the actual encounter of radically different convictions about questions of ultimate meaning.

Perhaps what we are looking for has been well captured by Ulrich Winkler's call for a 'comparative theology of religions': an attempt to do theology *with* one another in the mode of comparison.[16] A growing store of authenticated knowledge, tested in multilateral comparison, can only strengthen the religions in what Christians call 'faith'. Despite all the evidence of mutual antagonism and scientific scepticism, there is no other foundation for the supreme human task of learning to live in peace on a habitable planet.

---

16   See Winkler, Ulrich, Editorial, in the issue of *Salzburger Theologische Zeitschrift* 11/2 (2007), 137-139, on the theme "Komparative Theologie der Religionen". Winkler's own contribution, "Für eine pneumatologische Religionstheologie", 175-200, is a conventional though innovative example of theology of religions from a Christian perspective.

8.2 Collaborative Theology

If comparative theology – reading and comparing texts of different traditions – is an *imagined* exchange of insights, then collaborative theology would be a *real* exchange with the purpose of actual intellectual and practical cooperation.[17] In many respects the two programs overlap: Clooney, too, envisages cooperation and mutual encouragement by the reading and reflecting theologians. But when one makes comparison alone the central concern, one elegantly sidesteps the sensitive question of religious pluralism. The fact that there are numerous religions which comparison shows to differ from one's own is made from the standpoint of one's own faith, which in the process may be complemented by new insights but at its core remains unshaken. But if one is really working with a partner from another tradition to identify and try to solve problems that are found to be common to both, one must be prepared to test and possibly question aspects of the meaning, truth content, and ethical orientation of one's own and the other's faith.

Some, for whom the search for a common basis appears merely 'modern', not rigorously 'post-modern', may find this unsatisfactory.[18] But in the situation created by global civil society with its constant information flows and ideological conflicts, it will not be enough simply to let religious differences be; they need to be actively and collaboratively engaged with in what one might call an interreligious theology or an interactive pluralism. It may well be that such a pluralistic coexistence is a more realistic goal

---

17   May, John D'Arcy, *Buddhologie und Christologie. Unterwegs zu einer kollaborativen Theologie* (Innsbruck-Wien: Tyrolia Verlag, 2014), 12-13.

18   Magliola, Robert, *Facing Up to Real Doctrinal Difference: How Some Motifs from Derrida can Nourish the Catholic-Buddhist Encounter* (Kettering, Ohio: Angelico Press, 2014); see my review, May, John D'Arcy, *Buddhist-Christian Studies* 35 (2015), 238-241.

than a prematurely constructed ultimate commonality which only intellectual elites can fully grasp.[19] Not all would put it as bluntly as Majid Tehranian: "The new Global Civilization demands a new faith. That faith has to transcend all existing faiths".[20] If a Muslim can assert this, then Christian theologians have much to ponder. One thing, at any rate, is clear: if we are even to approximate to these goals, we must all change the way we do theology.

Does this imply relativism? Not necessarily. Relativism, in the end, is self-contradictory, because it destroys any basis for certain knowledge. But convinced adherents of different religions, even radically different ones, who engage in discussion about their differences are nevertheless firmly convinced of their respective ways of believing and will in all probability remain so. It is nevertheless possible and even desirable, as many examples show, that they go forward together to make explicit new perspectives which were not recognised up till then in both their traditions.

This step has methodological presuppositions which are not yet entirely clear. One is that, unlike the case of comparative religion, one is not working with a concept of religion 'in general', as if this were clear *before* one investigates particular traditions. A second is that, unlike the theology of religions, one may not presuppose one's own traditions and convictions as normative and ultimately immune from criticism. But an unquestioning acceptance of pluralism is not adequate either, because in that case a previously constructed theory is made the framework of interreligious reflection.

---

19   See Chakravarti Ram-Prasad, "Response to Engineer", Ridgeon, Lloyd and Perry Schmidt-Leukel, eds, *Islam and Inter-Faith Relations* (London: SCM, 2007), 209.

20   Tehranian, Majid, "A Muslim View of Buddhism", Ridgeon and Schmidt-Leukel, *Islam and Inter-Faith Relations*, 213-224, 216.

Theological collaboration is thus more likely to be facilitated when the participants first of all bear witness to their own faiths, well knowing that these traditionally include claims to absoluteness and exclusiveness. In a genuine dialogue, one must learn to deal with these. Testing their validity belongs to the central tenets of any theology. Even where there is no *theos*, as in Buddhism, or an overwhelming abundance of gods, as in Hinduism, or a diffuse 'sacredness' with multiple manifestations, as in Shinto, it is possible to recognise the sense in which the faithful acknowledge a transcendent reality and adopt corresponding attitudes. We have seen how shocked the first missionaries in the Pacific were when they realised that there was no transcendent God in the myths and rituals of these peoples, yet from a gradual coming together of the apparently so widely disparate standpoints there emerged new and promising theologies, ones that deserve the name, even if they are no longer conceived in Western Christian terms.[21] Those who, like Paul Knitter, practise religious 'double belonging' go far beyond comparison to participate intellectually and ritually in the 'other' tradition.[22]

There are also historical obstacles standing in the way of collaborative theology which are not easily overcome. Christianity in particular made its way into the Asia-Pacific with such powerful resources and claims to universal validity – the exclusive truth of Christian teachings, the moral superiority of Christian ethics –

---

21   May, John D'Arcy, *Christus Initiator. Theologie im Pazifik* (Düsseldorf: Patmos, 1990 = Theologie Interkulturell 4); Trompf, Garry W., *Melanesian Religion* (Cambridge: Cambridge University Press, 1991).

22   Knitter, Paul F., *Without Buddha I Could Not Be a Christian* (Oxford und New York: OneWorld, 2009); see also Goosen, Gideon, *Hyphenated Christians: Towards a Better Understanding of Dual Religious Belonging* (Bern: Peter Lang, 2011); Drew, Rose, *Buddhist and Christian? An Exploration of Dual Belonging* (London und New York: Routledge, 2011); May, John D'Arcy, ed., *Converging Ways? Conversion and Belonging in Buddhism and Christianity* (St Ottilien: EOS Verlag, 2007).

that it leaves a legacy of mutual resentment which must first of all be worked through before a constructive theological conversation can even begin. Hinduism lives on in the cultural substratum of indigenous cultures in Malaysia and Indonesia, though Islam is now by far the majority in both countries. But on closer inspection, as we have seen, tensions between the primal religious traditions of these peoples and the absolute claims of Islam remain. Buddhism, too, despite centuries of inculturation, was branded a foreign religion in certain historical periods in China and Japan and was persecuted. Even in 'Buddhist countries' like Myanmar or Thailand, Buddhism subsists in a kind of uneasy symbiosis with people's native religion. There is thus much 'theological' work to be done, even internally, if traditions that exist alongside or interpenetrate one another are to be capable of collaboration.

I call this the 'immanent hermeneutic' which every community that incorporates a tradition must constantly practise if it is to reappropriate and understand its own identity in new circumstances, to cultivate it and pass it on to future generations. But under the conditions of religious pluralism, as we have repeatedly seen, it is just as important for the religious community as a 'system' to maintain reciprocal relations with its 'environment' (to use terms coined by the German sociologist Niklas Luhmann). This demands much more than mere politeness *ad extra* and judgments according to one's private criteria *ad intra*. Interreligious relationships, whatever their context, are not simply 'foreign policy', but – to borrow a term used by the German philosopher Carl Friedrich von Weizsäcker – *Weltinnenpolitik* ('global domestic policy').

What this amounts to is that in the global civil society presently taking shape, abstract pluralism becomes collaborative action and reflection on faith – no longer in the isolation of putative orthodoxy but in constant conversation with one's respective 'others'. The business of comparison as the spur to better self-knowledge thus becomes active cooperation, especially in the areas of spiritual and intellectual sharing. In many places, for example in relations between Buddhist and Christians or Muslims and Hindus, such cooperation is already under way, despite tensions and conflicts.

8.3 Global Theology?

In the twentieth century, there were many attempts to formulate a 'world theology', though they were far in advance of the actual relationships between religions. The most impressive was perhaps the historically well founded achievement of Wilfred Cantwell Smith, whose humane person-centred approach to interreligious relations makes it stand out even today, though it was contested at the time.[23] These projects demonstrate just how complex the elaboration of a truly global theology would be.[24] For Smith, such a global theology was feasible only if suitably informed representatives of religious traditions learned to do theology collaboratively, and he even gave an informal and amusing sketch of how such collaboration might work.[25] In a certain analogy to the

---

[23] Smith, Wilfred Cantwell, *Towards a World Theology: Faith and the Comparative History of Religion* (London: Macmillan, 1981); see also May, John D'Arcy, "The Globalisation of Theology", Price, Peter, ed., *A World United or a World Exploited? Christian Perspectives on Globalisation* (Adelaide: Australian Theological Forum, 2013 = *Interface* 16/2), 64-80; *id.*, "Political Religion: Secularity and the Study of Religion in Global Civil Society", Basia Spalek and Alia Imtoual, eds, *Religion, Spirituality and the Social Sciences: Challenging Marginalisation* (Bristol: Policy Press, 2008), 9-22.

[24] See, for example, Swidler, Leonard, *After the Absolute: The Dialogical Future of Religion* (Minneapolis: Fortress Press, 1990); *id.*, ed., *Toward a Universal Theology of Religion* (Maryknoll: Orbis Books, 1987); Reat, N. Ross and E. Perry, *A World Theology: The Central Spiritual Reality of Humankind* (Cambridge: Cambridge University Press, 1991).

[25] Smith, *World Theology*, Chapter 7.

situation of nation states in the face of globalisation, the religions are confronted by the puzzle of how they, when each in its own way claims absoluteness, could belong to a religious world order whose parameters they no longer define. To solve this puzzle, a first minimal step might be to ascertain the ethical basis on which they could deal with the problems and prejudices of a world becoming one yet at the same time riven by absolutisms in conflict.

Perhaps the most lasting achievement of Hans Küng is to have pointed the way to this resolution with his development of a 'global ethic' to which the (great, 'universal') religions could contribute.[26] The drawback of such an initiative is that it sets before radically different religions an extraneous schema within which they are invited to locate their particularities. Not all felt able to do this, although – or perhaps because – the schema was deliberately kept as open as possible. The religions have resources peculiar to each on which they can draw to resolve conflicts and formulate their own moral standpoints, all of which could enrich the pluralism of values. As in the case of economic development, however, patience is called for: we are dealing with traditions thousands of years old. Their narratives are based on symbolic contents whose translation into language which remains true to the convictions of the faithful, and at the same time proves viable and legitimate in the communication networks of global civil society, will be accompanied by struggles and resistance. It is encouraging that religious communities, from the Roman Catholic Church in Vatican II to Japanese Shinto, even progressive circles in Islam and representatives of primal traditions, are ready to take first steps in this direction. These movements are creating, not a static

---

26 Küng, Hans, *Projekt Weltethos* (München-Zürich: Piper, 1990); see also May, John D'Arcy, *After Pluralism: Towards an Interreligious Ethic* (Münster-Hamburg-London: LIT Verlag, 2000); Sullivan, William M., and Will Kymlicka, eds, *The Globalization of Ethics* (Cambridge: Cambridge University Press, 2007).

intellectual, but an *interactive* pluralism, in which differences can at once be recognised and overcome, without loss of identity but with considerable gain in plausibility.

This is already happening, but it doesn't always carry the label 'collaborative theology'. In Australia, a 'rainbow spirit theology' was conceived by the Rainbow Spirit Elders in collaboration with sympathetic white theologians. In Melanesia, examples began to appear in the dissertations presented at the theological colleges and in the pages of the *Melanesian Journal of Theology*. We have seen how Asian theologians, whether Buddhist, Christian or Muslim, have approached their opposite numbers in the other faiths in order to reformulate their theologies. It is not generally realised that, throughout the Middle Ages, Muslims were much better informed about other religions and more objective in their judgments of them than Christians.[27] Progressive Buddhist thinkers such as Thich Nhat Hanh, the Dalai Lama and the Thai monk Buddhadasa have explored the possibilities of a Buddhist 'inclusivism', utilising traditional concepts such as the all-inclusive 'one vehicle' (*ekayana*) of the *Lotus Sutra* or the theory of 'two truths', a transcendent truth (*paramartha-satya*) which is knowable to liberated ones but inaccessible to reason, and a conventional truth (*samvrti-satya*) which is valid in the everyday life-world constructed by language.

Many who are working intensively in the field of interreligious studies are beginning to realise that we need to go beyond objective surveys of the ways the religions represent themselves in the public sphere to the point where they begin to engage with one another theologically. In the case of Christianity and Islam, Martin Bauschke can assert:

---

[27] See Ridgeon, Lloyd and Perry Schmidt-Leukel, editors' introduction, *Islam and Inter-Faith Relations* (London: SCM, 2007), 3, citing the view of Harold Coward and referring to more detailed research by Jacques Waardenburg.

In face of fundamentalist demagogues both sides have the responsibility to create an alternative to ... a 'theology of hate', that is, a *theology of reconciliation and friendship between Christians and Muslims*. This theology needs to be developed jointly and, being a common Christian-Muslim theology, it is therefore different from either a 'Christian view of Islam' or a 'Muslim view of Christianity' as we have presented here.[28]

Any such venture, of course, has presuppositions which are only just beginning to be explored; as Bauschke continues:

In order to develop a Christian-Muslim theology of reconciliation and friendship we need a *common Christian-Muslim hermeneutics of their sacred Scriptures*.[29]

Remarking on how teachings such as 'skilful means' (*kausalya-upaya*) have allowed Buddhists to assimilate viewpoints from other schools while maintaining the doctrinal superiority of their own, John Makransky acknowledges that

Buddhist traditions of Asia, and now of the West, are products of the recurrent, fresh integration of non-Buddhist religious and cultural elements into new Buddhist frameworks.[30]

---

[28] Bauschke, "Response to Siddiqui", Ridgeon and Schmidt-Leukel, *Islam and Inter-Faith Relations*, 159 (emphasis in original).

[29] Bauschke, "Response to Siddiqui", Ridgeon and Schmidt-Leukel, *Islam and Inter-Faith Relations*, 161 (emphasis in original).

[30] Makransky, John, "Buddhist Inclusivism: Reflections Toward a Contemporary Buddhist Theology of Religions", Schmidt-Leukel, Perry, ed., *Buddhist Attitudes to Other Religions* (St Ottilien: EOS Verlag, 2008), 47-68, 59.

Agreeing with Catholic theologian Jacques Dupuis that religions need one another in order to plumb the depths of their own truths, Makransky goes on:

> It is not just that Buddhahood is speaking itself through other religious traditions so as to include them as lower levels of preparation on the ladder to Buddhist enlightenment. Rather Buddhists *need* the wisdom of religious others to help disclose to them what lies outside of the historically conditioned limitations of their own tradition, to help them receive *more* of the truth that frees, perhaps sometimes in surprising and unexpected ways…[31]

In developing what he unapologetically calls a Buddhist *theology*, notwithstanding the absence of a personal God in traditional Buddhist thought, Makransky freely acknowledges the influence on him of Christian colleagues such as the Jesuit Francis Clooney.

Perhaps it is now more apparent that 'communication' is the indispensable mediator between 'comparison' and 'collaboration'. My colleague John Dupuche tells how, when he is in India, he is not asked 'What do you believe?' but 'What have you experienced?' Spiritual experience, shared in face-to-face conversation, will be the fundamental medium of collaborative theology, or we could speak of 'comparative experience' as the bridge from comparative to interreligious theology. This may be daunting for the more doctrinally developed religions such as Christianity and Buddhism, in which the questioning of fundamentals appears to threaten whole doctrinal edifices erected over the centuries to safeguard central beliefs. But those who have entered into such

---

31   Makransky, "Buddhist Inclusivism", 64.

conversations with openness to new insights and trust in their own fidelity and their partners' integrity regularly report that they have been liberated from culturally conditioned narrowness and inspired to renewed faithfulness to what really matters in their respective heritages.

The outcome of such reciprocal engagement is not knowable in advance; to embark on it demands a special kind of courage, which is more likely to be found among lonely pioneers than the hierarchies of religious authority. But if theology – now of an intercultural and interreligious type[32] – is to keep pace with the breathtaking developments of globalisation, the construction of such theology, shared among all traditions willing to participate, would seem to be the true ecumenical alternative to ethnocentrism and religious absolutism.

The religions are not merely 'systems' within the larger system of global awareness, they are *autopoietic* systems (Heinz-Günther Stobbe, drawing on the ideas of Niklas Luhmann). Their identity construction is an internal process consisting of continually rediscovering themselves in the act of marking themselves off from others, yet it needs awareness of others and interaction with them. This need not mean excluding the others, because this constant activity of self-constitution takes place in the communicative flows of global civil society. The more the different religions become aware of their respective 'others', the more intense will the process of constructing and maintaining identity become within the overall process of interactive pluralism. Remaining themselves, they will all be invited – or constrained – to reflect *together* on the implications of their interrelationships. In thinking these through

---

32 See May, John D'Arcy, and Linda Hogan, "Visioning Ecumenics as Intercultural, Inter-religious, and Public Theology", Linda Hogan, Solange Lefebvre, Norbert Hintersteiner, Felix Wilfred, eds, *Concilium: From World Mission to Inter-religious Witness* (London: SCM, 2011), 70-81.

they will in effect be doing theology together, each yielding elements of its autonomy-in-isolation to the others.

We should not underestimate the degree of *metanoia* (spiritual and intellectual conversion) this will demand, both from the guardians of orthodoxy and from the individual faithful. This will not be a matter either of an abstract, universal 'religion in general' or of fundamentalist clinging to inherited beliefs. The balancing act required will be difficult and risky; but it is indispensable, if global civil society is to be based not only on ethical but on spiritual values. Values are very concrete orientations, both ethical and aesthetic. Meddling with them can neutralise them and rob them of their power. This is precisely what seems to be happening as values become detached from their roots in particular traditions in the virtual networks of global electronic communication. In attempting to work against this, the religions risk appearing to be reactionary and conservative. But without the religions, a global civil society is inconceivable. The ecumenical task, to which we must now turn our attention, is to ensure that the religions shape the public sphere constructively, not destructively.

Chapter 9: The Ecumenical Imperative

Our topic has two sides: the fate of the religions in the emerging global civil society, and the fate of the global order itself (the much-touted 'international rules-based order') in its rapid evolution towards technopolis accompanied by the rise of populist parties, terrorist movements and rogue states. I have been at pains to show that these are two sides of the same coin: without a new alignment of the religions there will be no *ethical* globalisation; and without ethically responsible globalisation we may expect a future of war (whether cold, trade or hot) and destruction. The many examples we have seen from the Asia-Pacific indicate how difficult it will be to turn the accelerating developments now under way in this direction.

In addition, many leading scientists and politicians are convinced that the religions have nothing at all to contribute to a future world order. Far from being part of the solution, with their absolute claims and constant quarrels they are a large part of the problem, causes rather than mediators of conflict. Others, equally influential, place the blame on *other* religions, never their own. Though token efforts are made to acknowledge interfaith dialogue, ecumenism is often looked upon with condescension, if not derision, by the power brokers, both secular and religious, who think they rule the world. Yet the task facing us is in the truest and original meaning of the word an *ecumenical* one, and in this concluding chapter we want to get to the bottom of what it really involves.

The Greek word *oikos* means not only 'house', but the household in its entirety. Running the household responsibly sustains the life of the domestic community and makes it fruitful.

Today we must learn to widen the scope of this idea to include not only the state, but the whole inhabited earth as the household of all humans and all living beings. This brings together three dimensions of communal living, all of which are derived from *oikos*, but whose interrelationships are almost never considered:

- *Economy*, the household of economics, finance and trade
- *Ecology*, the household of climate and the natural world
- *Ecumenism*, the household of ethical values and the religions

The key point is that human beings alone are capable of grasping these interrelationships and their implications for all living things and their natural environment. This awareness should result in our taking responsibility for global housekeeping that is economically and ecologically sustainable, to the benefit of all. Christian theology (and by implication the theologies of other religions) must therefore be pursued from now on in two interrelated dimensions, which again are seldom connected:

1. *Intercultural and interreligious*, the interactive religious pluralism we have already explained
2. *International and political*, having regard to the global public sphere in which a global civil society is taking shape

Together these amount to a 'cosmopolitan' perspective.[1] The task, then, is to reconceive the ecumenical in all its dimensions as an alternative to the ethnocentrism, nationalism and exclusivism we see hardening all around us. In other words, as the French

---

1 Appiah, Kwame Anthony, *Cosmopolitanism: Ethics in a World of Strangers* (London: Allen Lane, 2006).

might say, *imaginons l'oecuménique?* The task is huge, of course, but it can better be seen in perspective if it is first tackled at home, or as the World Council of Churches put it (New Delhi, 1961), by 'all in each place'; for if mutual understanding, agreement and peacebuilding do not happen *locally*, they can hardly be expected to take root *globally*.³

This perspective roughly corresponds to the tension between 'cosmopolitanism' and 'communitarianism' in international relations theory. It may be correlated with the interesting comparison developed by David Goodhart between 'Anywheres', people whose education and social advantages allow them to move easily in foreign countries and international institutions, and 'Somewheres', those who prefer to remain rooted in the familiar surroundings of their place of birth.⁴ Modern Europe has inherited from the Enlightenment the universalistic tradition of Kant, which was foreshadowed by the Medieval theory of natural law and is still recognisable in the thinking of Habermas or Rawls.

In this perspective, moral obligation is derived from the unique value of each human individual. Ethical systems may be determined by particular contexts, but ethics itself takes priority

---

2   May, John D'Arcy, *Imagining the Ecumenical: A Personal Journey* (Northcote, Vic.: Morning Star, 2016); *id.*, "Die ökumenische Alternative. Die eine bewohnte Erde neu denken", *Salzburger Theologische Zeitschrift* 14/2 (2010), 187-202; Cobb, John B., *Sustainability: Economics, Ecology and Justice* (Maryknoll: Orbis Books, 1992); Humphreys, Stephen, *Climate Change and Human Rights: A Rough Guide* (Geneva: International Council on Human Rights Policy, 2008).

3   May, John D'Arcy, "'All in Each Place': Buddhist-Christian Relations at Home and Abroad", *Postscriptum* to Schmidt-Leukel, Perry, ed., *Buddhist-Christian Relations in Asia* (Sankt Ottilien: EOS Verlag, 2017), 429-444.

4   Goodhart, David, *The Road to Somewhere: The New Tribes Shaping British Politics* (Melbourne: Penguin Random House, 2017). Goodhart is endeavoring to explain the great political disruptions of the Brexit referendum and the election of Trump. On the following see Atack, Iain, *The Ethics of Peace and War: From State Security to World Community* (Edinburgh: Edinburgh University Press, 2005), Chapter 4.

over the moral claims of states and cultural communities, because it is intrinsically egalitarian and universal. Each human being, regardless of ethnicity or religion, deserves the same recognition and respect. Civil society, which acknowledges the autonomy of individual citizens with regard to the state, can thus be the forerunner of a *global* civil society, which must be by definition *cosmopolitan*, because the rights and duties that characterise it are valid for *all* people, regardless of origin. "Global civil society thus provides a normative and institutional basis for cosmopolitanism that is distinct from the state and conventional state sovereignty".[5] Of course, as Goodhart reminds us, in real life societies matters are not so straightforward: those materially affected by globalisation are still in a minority, and cosmopolitan attitudes are largely confined to educated elites. Correspondingly, churchgoers and members of other religious communities tend to prioritise their own familiar liturgical and doctrinal ambience over the demands of ecumenical openness.

Nevertheless, the new situation demands a truly ecumenical theology which integrates all these dimensions so as to be able to influence science, economics and politics through the medium of ethics. Under the conditions pertaining in the public spheres of pluralistic societies, this can only happen if the religions are in a position to argue rationally for their beliefs and demonstrate them by an ethical way of living.[6] They must learn to include the 'third partner', the human and natural sciences, in every *interreligious*

---

5   Atack, *Ethics of Peace and War*, 49, referring to Mary Kaldor.
6   Herschock, Peter D., *Buddhism in the Public Sphere: Reorienting Global Interdependence* (London und New York: Routledge, 2006); see the review by Loy, David R., *Philosophy East and West* 58/1 (2008), 144-147. See also: Gascoigne, Robert, *The Public Forum and Christian Ethics* (Cambridge: Cambridge University Press, 2001); *id.*, "Christian Faith and the Public Forum in a Pluralist Society", *Colloquium* 26.2 (1994), 116-120; Coleman, John A., and William F. Ryan, eds, *Globalization and Catholic Social Thought: Present Crisis, Future Hope* (Maryknoll: Orbis, 2005).

dialogue. This means that collaborative theologies would be by definition *interdisciplinary*. It also implies that the religions must be credible *in their plurality*; that their relationships to one another must exemplify what they are recommending to the international community. It is self-evident that we are a long way from this.

In other words: the solution of the problem of religious and theological pluralism is in the first instance *ethical*, and questions concerning the truth of their various teachings can only be discussed on this basis. Doctrinal matters cannot be compared and correlated to the mutual satisfaction of those participating in dialogue unless the fundamental ethical values of mutual respect and recognition of one another's religious and spiritual qualities come into play. Interreligious relations must demonstrate the ethical quality demanded of international relations: they must be capable of accommodating plurality. This process is already under way, both in high level initiatives (the Declaration on Non-Christian Religions of Vatican II, *Nostra Aetate*, 28 October 1965; the Muslim manifesto *A Common Word*, 13 October 2007; the Jewish statement *Dabru emet*, 10 September 2000) and in numerous local contexts.

What we find throughout the Asia-Pacific, however, is an ecumenism conceived and structured (and often enough financially supported) by the West. The perennial problem of such 'official' ecumenism is that, because it is largely in the hands of professional ecumenists, it evinces little interest in local communities of whatever faith. This is a serious deficiency, because only when faith communities come together and cooperate at local level, overcome their misunderstandings and anxieties and get to know one another from the inside, can they credibly influence a wider public sphere, whether religious or political. It is encouraging that such grass roots activity in particular places can more easily become known in wider circles, even internationally, thanks to today's communications media. It is characteristic of civil society that this networking can bypass the official bodies of religions and states. 'Base' groups and movements thus acquire an autonomy that can seem threatening to hierarchies and authorities, but is indispensable if civil society's capacity for action is to be exploited to the full.

This freedom of movement also makes it possible for ecumenical attitudes and collaborative theological effort, if not like a bushfire, then at least like glowing coals to ignite interreligious activities in various countries simultaneously. We have seen sufficient evidence of how huge this task is: Buddhist-Hindu conflicts in Sri Lanka, Muslim-Hindu conflicts in India, the Buddhist persecution of Muslims in Myanmar, Muslim atrocities against Christians in Indonesia, Evangelical and Protestant tensions with Catholics in the Pacific Islands, Sunni-Shi'a violence in Indonesia, religious indifferentism and militant atheism in Australia… the list is long.

Instead of investing time and effort in such conflicts, incomprehensible to outsiders, convinced ecumenists would rather see the religions, together in each place, dedicating themselves to solving the region's real problems: spiritual emptiness, cultural alienation, social inequality, financial corruption, environmental destruction, poverty, refugees… this list, too, is long. The potential for the religions to be effective is all the more evident in that political divisions increasingly tend to be cultural rather than economic.

All these problems have a spiritual dimension which mostly remains invisible. It is this that we now wish to bring to light while recapitulating our main findings. We shall first return to our original question of fear of democracy and the widening of civil society (9.1). We shall then raise the question of responsible economics – beginning with the sustainability of agriculture – in relation to culture and religion (9.2). In conclusion, we hope to have progressed to the point where we can make credible the mutual enrichment inherent in ecumenical cooperation, whether in action or in theology (9.3).

9.1 Democracy as the Institutionalisation of Justice

It should by now be sufficiently clear that democracy is not necessarily secular or even liberal, not to mention Western, in order to give widely diverse peoples the freedoms and opportunities to guarantee a worthwhile human existence. We also saw that democracy in many ways has religious roots. It is evident, however, that under ideological influences, whether they be ethnic and racial or religious and nationalistic, democracy can be perverted till all that remains is the hollow shell of an authoritarian system; hence the term 'illiberal democracy' applied to countries like Turkey, Myanmar or the Philippines, and claimed perhaps most outrageously by the Hungarian leader Viktor Orban. In the end, democracy is a pragmatic affair, 'the worst system of government, with the exception of all the others', as Churchill famously put it. In its various forms – always needing improvement, always having to be fought for – it *can* come close to satisfying the needs of citizens.

As we have repeatedly seen, the indispensable precondition of any democracy is a functioning civil society; where this is absent (think of the difficulties facing civil society in China, Russia or Turkey) democratic institutions are merely a façade. It is equally obvious that there can be no functioning *global* civil society without spaces for democratic freedom at national and local level, which make it possible to form opinion and critique the political process. Examples such as India, Japan or Taiwan show, however, that democratic pluralism need not be structured on a Western model. More recently, a truly striking irony is becoming apparent: a quarter century after the fall of the Berlin wall and the return to democracy in East Germany (*die Wende*), new walls are being erected around many democratic countries: between Israel and Palestine (700 km), India and Bangladesh (3,800 km), the USA and Mexico (3,200 km), the EU and the Balkan states – and where physical walls are impracticable, e.g. around the island continent of Australia, legal barriers are erected. This has been called 'barricade democracy'.[7] The practice is diametrically opposed to the very notion of a global civil society.

We recall the account of the fundamental crisis of democracy during the turbulent period of the Weimar Republic, when the Catholic jurist Carl Schmitt (1888-1985) doubted whether liberalism could be the unconditional basis of a democratic order (3.3). He developed a 'political theology' in which the state does not derive from a social contract, but from the popular sovereignty that makes such a contract possible. Religion, far from being a 'private matter', as liberal theory supposes, is the foundation of political experience. Sovereignty accrues to whoever decides in the face of the exceptional case. The exception is not the norm; the norm serves only to identify the exception. The decision about the exception is an act of will equivalent to an act of faith. Only this guarantees freedom. The state may not rely on legally codified norms; beyond all norms it is constantly willing itself into existence.

Democracy is thus in no sense normative. Every 'exception', every existential threat to the political order must continually

---

[7] Triffitt, Mark, "Beware of Democracy's Retreat behind Walls", *The Age* (Melbourne), 14/3/2016.

be met with the call to commitment and sacrifice. In Schmitt's opinion, liberal theory does not even recognise the problem: that democracy on a liberal basis can be abolished by forces from within and without. In the face of emerging fascism, this was the case; and present-day challenges to democracy such as Islamism, global warming or the refugee crisis show that such dangers still exist. Schmitt's personal decision was ultimately wrong, but his fundamental principle, that democracy is not identical to liberalism, gives us food for thought in view of the weaknesses becoming apparent in democracies East and West.[8]

Globalisation has been characterised as ideally a 'democracy of democracies'.[9] We have seen how democracies can deviate widely from European norms, and there is no precedent for the meta-democracy they are supposed to constitute. For this very reason, the development of a global civil society is so important. The idea of a global public sphere is difficult to conceive in a time of the competing superpowers China and America, numerous conflicts within and between states and the rise of Muslim-inspired counter-movements such as al-Qaida, the Taliban and Islamic State. But it is equally true that it is this world situation, riddled with conflict and unrest, that drives the emergence of a global civil sphere. The democracies themselves are slowly being transformed by the demands of these international tensions in the direction of a global, not just national responsibility: they are becoming cosmo-politan.

---

8   Miller, Nick, "Dawn of the Demagogues: Is Democracy Winning or Losing the Global Contest?", *The Sunday Age*, 25/2/2018, discussing recent books such as *How Democracies Die* by Steven Levitsky and Daniel Ziblatt and the somewhat more optimistic view of Steven Pinker, *Enlightenment Now.*

9   Held, David, "Democracy: From City-states to a Cosmopolitan Order?", *id.*, ed., *Prospects for Democracy: North, South, East, West* (Cambridge: Polity Press, 1993), 13-52.

The refusal of the 'Visegrad Four' (Poland, Slovakia, Hungary and the Czech Republic) and other members of the European Union, not to mention Australia and the United States, to admit refugees desperately seeking asylum illustrates the pressures the democracies are under and the dangers of reacting in a heartless and authoritarian manner. Goodhart reminds us that it was the enthusiastic acceptance of immigration and multiculturalism by his 'Anywhere' class of educated elites, without much regard for the anxieties this caused among the 'Somewheres' with their ties to national identity and local community, which led to the revolt of Brexit and the election of Trump.[10]

Democracy is, above all, a tradition, an ancient and many-sided one, as we have seen, but nevertheless recognisable as a particular way of life and form of government which has undergone many developments, has sometimes all but disappeared but has always revived.[11] Although in its Western forms it is based on strongly individualistic and secularistic presuppositions, in its origins it is just as strongly religious in character. The first freedom that was fought for and won as modern democracies established themselves was freedom of belief for individuals and religious liberty in the legal provisions of states.[12] Although it would seem to be in their own interest, the religions, because of their absolute claims and privileges, have often been reluctant to come to terms with the freedoms that pluralism guarantees; we may think of the battles to pass the Declaration on Religious Liberty of Vatican II, *Dignitatis Humanae* (1965), or the religious control of all aspects

---

10   Goodhart, *The Road to Somewhere*, Chapter 4. Others have contrasted 'kin' and 'cosmopolis' (Nigel Biggar) or 'nationalism' and 'globalism'.

11   Stout, Jeffrey, *Democracy and Tradition* (Princeton-Oxford: Princeton University Press, 2004); Keane, John, *The Life and Death of Democracy* (London-Sydney-New York-Toronto: Pocket Books [Simon and Schuster], 2009).

12   Reynolds, Noel B., und W. Cole Durham Jr., eds, *Religious Liberty in Western Thought* (Atlanta: Scholars Press, 1996).

of life in Saudi Arabia and such democratic institutions as there are in Iran. The challenge to the religions to be forces for social and ecological justice lies precisely here. As John de Gruchy has said, democracy is not only a system, but in the first instance a vision. The religions are similar: they do indeed offer humanity an ethic of survival, but only because more fundamentally they incorporate a vision of hope.[13]

Democracy as a system is always the outcome of a struggle to make the vision reality. It is much more than simply the right to vote; it is rather a constant search for justice by politically engaged individuals and institutions in which they can participate.[14] As the conscious exercise of responsibility in participatory community life, democracy is by no means weak, but ecological destruction and ethnic-religious nationalism can undermine it unless civil society counteracts them.[15] The protests of the French population after the attacks of Islamic State in 2015 is a remarkable example of this, but the reaction of the French government – an ongoing state of emergency – also shows that the putative protection of democratic freedoms can bring about their abolition. The German Chancellor Angela Merkel's generosity towards refugees in the same year led to the rise of anti-immigrant parties such as *Alternative für Deutschland* and a crisis of her coalition government in 2018. Australian politics have also been poisoned by the unresolved situation of asylum seekers kept in indefinite offshore detention on Manus and Nauru. The religions can only contribute to the

---

13   De Gruchy, John, *Christianity and Democracy: A Theology for a Just World Order* (Cambridge: Cambridge University Press, 1995); Clark, John, *Worlds Apart: Civil Society and the Battle for Ethical Globalization* (London: Earthscan Publications, 2003); May, John D'Arcy, "Ethic of Survival or Vision of Hope? The Aim of Interreligious Dialogue", *Dharma World* 29 (Sept.-Oct. 2002), 25-28.

14   De Gruchy, *Christianity and Democracy*, 21.

15   De Gruchy, *Christianity and Democracy*, 237, 247-248, 260-261.

strengthening of civil society if they do so together, overcoming their fear of pluralism and taking the risk of theological and political collaboration. Here is the core of the ecumenical task that is at the heart of this study.

9.2 Ecumenical Religion and Economics

No political system or ideology can survive unless there is a material basis for human life in the natural environment. The destruction of nature, justified by purely economic arguments, has become one of the most important issues of our time. It is not always appreciated that this also has a spiritual dimension which can easily be mistaken for mere idealism and romanticism.[16] 'Nature', as we have seen, is an extremely ambivalent concept, designating on the one hand the object of scientific investigation as expressed in mathematics, but on the other hand a metaphor for human sensibilities and feelings. It is entirely legitimate – indeed, it is the subject of all poetry – to seek in nature images of human sufferings and passions; a powerful but seldom used argument for the conservation of nature is that it is a source of such images.[17]

For Western Christian sensibilities, however, it is difficult to see nature not only as an object or a symbol, but as the subject of rights, with intrinsic value, quite independently of what it 'means' to people or whether it provides a basis for life.[18] The insight of

---

[16] The Australian agricultural scientist with long experience in Thailand, Lindsay Falvey, analyses this relationship with remarkable perspicuity, Falvey, Lindsay, *Religion and Agriculture: Sustainability in Christianity and Buddhism* (Adelaide: Institute for International Development, 2005).

[17] Collins, Paul, *Judgment Day: The Struggle for Life on Earth* (Sydney: University of New South Wales Press, 2010).

[18] May, John D'Arcy, "'Rights of the Earth' and 'Care for the Earth': Two Paradigms for a Buddhist-Christian Ecological Ethic", *Horizons* 21 (1994), 48-61; *id.*, "Human Dignity, Human Rights, and Religious Pluralism: Buddhist and Christian Perspectives", *Buddhist-Christian Studies* 26 (2006), 51-60; for the

indigenous and Asian religions, conveyed in different ways, that all natural phenomena, including the human, are fundamentally interdependent, complicates matters for well-intentioned ecologists who wish to defend responsible use of resources and sustainable agriculture against industries based purely on profit-making, but it also offers a perspective that goes well beyond merely legal and technical solutions.

The relationship between culture and agriculture, environment and civilisation immediately concerns the religions. We are sufficiently acquainted with the ways in which land and physical life are fundamentally important mediators of religious ideas and values (Chapter 5). Contrary to the prevailing opinion in Western or Western educated circles, religion is not an obsolete superstition that is gradually disappearing under the onslaught of rational criticism. For the vast majority of humankind it is central in the life of individuals and society and anchored in very particular places. The fact that we are dealing with extremely diverse expressions of religion according to particularities of place and culture is by no means always as problematic as it may appear in Western eyes. Often, even in Muslim countries like Indonesia and more so in Buddhist ones such as Japan, people 'belong' to several religions traditions simultaneously without being unduly troubled. Elsewhere, however, especially where the monotheistic religions predominate, religious sectarianism creates conflicts which can lead to prolonged violence.

This very violence is one of the main causes of the environmental degradation and refugee flows which condition one another and cause further deterioration in living standards. It has become one of the main objections to religion as such that it

---

historical background see Nash, Roderick F., *The Rights of Nature: A History of Environmental Ethics* (Madison: University of Wisconsin Press, 1989).

causes violence and persecution. The many examples of dialogue and co-operation among religions aimed at preserving the environment and accepting refugees attract much less attention. But these exist. They arise from the deepest convictions of people with widely differing beliefs (including atheists!) and show that mutual understanding across religious boundaries is certainly possible, not only as a pragmatic agreement in the face of urgent problems, but as a value in itself.

This is something quite different from the theoretical liberalism or pluralism so favoured by Western intellectuals, including Christians. Such understanding involves more than mere tolerance of other worldviews, which is rightly highly regarded in democratic societies. This approach can give the impression that the religions are being functionalised as a last desperate mobilisation of resources to fend off the looming disasters of ecological degradation and destructive wars. But, on closer inspection, such a tactical deployment of the religions by outside operators makes no sense. Religious traditions have a deeply rooted autonomy which they are not prepared to subordinate to demands for dialogue and co-operation from professional ecumenists or politicians. Nor is there any implication that, in the end, they are all 'the same'. They are not, and working through their differences while preserving their autonomy is the ecumenical task in a nutshell.

We are witnessing the deepening and widening of the religious convictions of so-called 'simple people', Goodhart's 'Somewheres' in religious contexts, despite inadequate education and deep-seated fear of the strange and foreign, to the point where they are able to come to terms with one another on all levels, emotionally, intellectually and culturally. Precisely this, whether in local contexts or beyond national boundaries and out into global civil society, is the substance of the ecumenical. Here we see how genuine ecumenical co-operation makes fundamental values real and operational, until people of different and even opposed faith orientations can acknowledge what they have in common. This concern for the essentials, life itself and the land that sustains it, contains an implicit criticism of the values that underlie the 'world religion' of the market and its 'theology', economics. From these sources counter-movements spring up which call into question capitalism and its excesses.[19]

Every economy is based on a philosophy that gives it its orientation, albeit implicitly. The presuppositions of the capitalist economic order involve options for very determinate conceptions of the human: that our material needs can in principle never be satisfied and must therefore be artificially stimulated over and over again to ensure that the production of goods continually grows. Underlying this is the assumption that competition among individuals to constantly produce and consume more is the rational basis of the economy, or, to put it more crassly, the economy is driven by egoism; 'greed is good'. That limitless consumption could have a very different – psychological and even spiritual – basis is not admitted as a valid argument. It does not enter into consideration that externalising the costs of this wasteful economic activity, which has consequences for the natural environment and people's health, does not appear on company balance sheets.

This is not only irrational, it flies in the face of the ethical convictions of the fathers of modern economics such as Adam Smith.[20] It can even be shown that in the most ancient mythical

---

19   Houtart, François, *Délégitimer le capitalisme. Reconstruire l'espérance* (Brüssel: Editions Colophon, 2005); Stiglitz, Joseph, *The Price of Inequality* (London: Allen Lane, 2012); Duchrow, Ulrich, *Alternatives to Global Capitalism: Drawn from Biblical History, Designed for Political Action* (Utrecht: International Books; Heidelberg, Kairos Europa, 1995).

20   Scherhorn, Gerhard, *Wachstum oder Nachhaltigkeit. Die Ökonomie am Scheideweg* (Erkelenz: Altius Verlag, 2015). Scherhorn draws on extensive

narratives of humankind and in classical philosophies the ethical foundations of trade are laid down, to reappear in distorted form in contemporary neo-liberalism, e.g. as the misguided theory of the 'invisible hand' that steers the market's lust for profit to the wellbeing of all.[21] In this context, the alleged contradiction of economy and ecology turns out to be the ideological justification of unlimited growth, i.e. profit maximisation. In the dynamics of global civil society this is a fundamental challenge to the ethical traditions of the religions.

9.3 Global Reflexivity

Confronted by people, or images of people, who are grieving after the loss of loved ones or traumatised by tragedies such as bushfires, floods or earthquakes, we don't need an interpreter to tell us what their tears or contorted expressions mean. The same applies to scenes of joy and celebration. These are human emotions we can all recognise; they are 'universal'. It is equally true, however, that such emotions are always expressed in cultural contexts which may assign them a status significantly different from what we might expect. Such contexts are powerfully reinforced by religious traditions, which interpret human suffering and earthly joy in quite different ways. This, in a nutshell, is the problem of universal and particular: to what extent can there be ethical norms, moral values, aesthetic principles and religious convictions that are truly universal, recognisable and acceptable for human beings anywhere and at any time?

---

empirical evidence to show that the legitimation of neo-liberal economies based on limitless consumption derives from false presuppositions.

21   Sedlacek, Thomas, *Economics of Good and Evil: The Quest for Economic Meaning from Gilgamesh to Wall Street* (New York: Oxford University Press, 2011).

When it comes to human rights, political freedoms and religious teachings, it is this purported universality that is ever more strongly contested in a world of competing economic systems deriving from ancient but contrasting ethical traditions. When it comes to making absolute truth claims for doctrines couched in the symbolism and terminology of very particular cultural origins, the religions are in the forefront. It is evident that under these circumstances the conditions for a global ethic supported by understanding and co-operation among the religions are very far from given, and with them the probability of a truly global civil society.

Abstract pluralism and liberal tolerance turn out to be, at most, preliminary steps towards the interreligious commitment that will be necessary if the dynamic of global civil society is to develop in the direction of a peaceful and environmentally stable world order. As we have seen, the main argument against religion of any kind in our day – no doubt made plausible by misunderstandings of the relationship between faith and reason, religion and science – is based on the observation that the religions appear to be the cause of violence, environmental destruction and persecution. It seems impossible to make credible that the religions, provided they remain true to their central teachings, make substantial contributions to care for the environment, the alleviation of suffering and the critique of exploitation – unless it becomes apparent that believers come to terms with one another's differences emotionally, culturally and intellectually to the point where their religious convictions are widened and deepened. This is not a matter of pragmatism, but a value in itself; it is nothing less than the substance of the ecumenical.

The thesis that pervades this study is that the emergence of a global civil society offers the religions hitherto unimagined possibilities of making real this ecumenical vision. In order to do so, they must cope with the paradox that the very truth convictions that give each of them their enduring identity and faith can become obstacles if they are made absolute in the isolation of defensive ideologies and institutions, instead of encountering the faith convictions of others interactively. In this situation, putative universality must be negotiated and striven for in collaboration with others, not taken for granted. Schweiker calls this interacting reflexively in a milieu of "global reflexivity".[22] This happens to the extent that the members of different faith communities and also, inasmuch as they exist, their 'official' institutions compare and cautiously begin to share the practical living out of their faiths, until they gain insight into one another's innermost religious convictions and spiritual riches.

This need not imply conversion: it can consist in reciprocal witness, or it can proceed to the stage of double religious belonging. It is this level of *praxis* that could give birth to the collaborative theology that will be necessary if these processes are to go ahead without misunderstandings, conflicts and sectarian rivalry. It then becomes possible to conceive of rapprochements that do not involve the betrayal of cherished traditions, but yield mutual enrichment.

---

22 Schweiker, William, *Theological Ethics and Global Dynamics: In the Time of Many Worlds* (Oxford: Blackwell, 2004), 157-158.

Bibliography

Ahrens, Theodor, "'Was ihr uns gebracht habt ist der Körper'. Erwägungen zur Frage, was Missionswissenschaft zur Erkenntnis Gottes beiträgt" [unpubl. Ms.]

Ahrens, Theodor, *Mission nachdenken. Studien* (Frankfurt: Lembeck, 2002)

Allen, John, *The Global War on Christians* (New York: Random House, 2013)

Appiah, Kwame Anthony, *Cosmopolitanism: Ethics in a World of Strangers* (London: Allen Lane, 2006)

Appleby, R. Scott, *The Ambivalence of the Sacred: Religion, Violence, and Reconciliation* (Lanham, Md.: Rowman & Littlefield, 2000)

Atack, Iain, *The Ethics of Peace and War: From State Security to World Community* (Edinburgh: Edinburgh University Press, 2005)

Augustine, Aurelius, *The City of God*, transl. Marcus Dods (New York: The Modern Library, 1950)

Australian Catholic Bishops' Conference, *For Those Who've Come Across the Seas: Justice for Refugees and Asylum Seekers*, Social Justice Statement 2015-16

Azra, A., "Militant Islamic Movements in Southeast Asia: Socio-political and Historical Contexts", *Kultur: The Indonesian Journal for Muslim Cultures* 3/1 (2003), 17-27

Azra, A., "The Challenge of Democracy in the Muslim World: Traditional Politics and Democratic Political Culture", K. Helmanita, I. Abubakar, D. Afianty, eds, *Dialogue in the World Disorder: A Response to the Threat of Unilateralism and World Terrorism* (Jakarta: Pusat Bahasa dan Budaya

Universitas Islam Negeri Syarif Hidayatulla Jakarta and Konrad Adenauer-Stiftung, 2004), 203-214

Bäumer, Remigius, ed., *Die Entwicklung des Konziliarismus. Werden und Nachwirkung der konziliaren Idee* (Darmstadt: Wissenschaftliche Buchgesellschaft, 1976)

Bauschke, Martin, "A Christian View of Islam", Ridgeon, Lloyd and Perry Schmidt-Leukel, eds, *Islam and Inter-Faith Relations* (London: SCM, 2007), 138-140.

Beasley, W.G., *The Japanese Experience: A Short History of Japan* (London: Phoenix Press, 2000)

Beck, Herman, *Les Musulmans d'Indonésie* (Turnhout: Éditions Brepols 2003)

Bellah, Robert N., Richard Madsen, William M. Sullivan, Ann Swidler, and Steven M. Tipton, *Habits of the Heart: Individualism and Commitment in American Life* (New York et al.: Harper & Row, 1986)

Berger, Peter, *The Desecularization of the World: Resurgent Religion and World Politics* (Washington, DC: Ethics and Public Policy Center; Grand Rapids: Eerdmans, 1999)

Berndt, Ronald M., and Catherine H. Berndt, *The Speaking Land: Myth and Story in Aboriginal Australia* (Ringwood: Penguin, 1988)

Beyer, Peter, *Religions in Global Society* (London and New York: Routledge, 2006)

Beyer, Ulrich, *Ein Volk zieht um. Indonesiens staatliches Umsiedlungsprogramm und die Kirchen* (Frankfurt: Lembeck, 1988)

Boff, Leonardo, *Global Civilization: Challenges to Society and Christianity* (London/Oakville: Equinox, 2005, orig. 2003)

Brennan, Frank, "Close the camps now and stop the posturing", *Eureka Street* 28/10 (2018)

Brewer, John D., "The Limits of Politics in Northern Ireland's Peace Process", in: John O'Grady, Cathy Higgins und Jude Lal Fernando, eds, *Mining Truths: Festschrift in Honour of Geraldine Smyth OP – Ecumenical Theologian and Peacebuilder* (St. Ottilien: EOS Verlag, 2015), 185-201

Brock, Peter, *Pacifism in Europe to 1914* (Princeton: Princeton University Press, 1972)

Brodbeck, Karl-Heinz, *Buddhistische Wirtschaftsethik. Eine Einführung* (Berlin: edition steinrich, 2002, rev. ed. 2011)

Buddhadasa, *Dhammic Socialism*, ed. Donald Swearer (Bangkok: Thai Inter-Religious Commission for Development, 1986)

Casanova, José, *Public Religions in the Modern World* (Chicago: University of Chicago Press, 1994)

Chappell, David W., ed., *Socially Engaged Spirituality: Essays in Honor of Sulak Sivaraksa on His 70th Birthday* (Bangkok: Sathirakoses-Nagapradipa Foundation, 2003)

Clark, John, *Worlds Apart: Civil Society and the Battle for Ethical Globalization* (London: Earthscan Publications, 2003)

Clooney, Francis X., "The Emerging Field of Comparative Theology: A Bibliographical Review (1889-1995)", *Theological Studies* 56 (1995), 521-550

Clooney, Francis X., *Komparative Theologie. Eingehendes Lernen über religiöse Grenzen hinweg* (Paderborn *et al.*: Schöningh, 2013)

Clooney, Francis, "Comparative Theology", in: *The Oxford Handbook of Systematic Theology* (Oxford: Oxford University Press, 2007), 653-669

Clooney, Francis, and Klaus von Stosch, eds, *How To Do Comparative Theology: Multiple Paths through Today's Field* (New York: Fordham University Press, 2017)

Clooney, Francis, *Hindu God, Christian God: How Reason Helps Break Down the Boundaries between Religions* (Oxford: Oxford University Press, 2001)

Cobb, John B., *Sustainability: Economics, Ecology and Justice* (Maryknoll: Orbis Books, 1992)

Coleman, John A., and William F. Ryan, eds, *Globalization and Catholic Social Thought: Present Crisis, Future Hope* (Maryknoll: Orbis, 2005)

Collins, Paul, *Judgment Day: The Struggle for Life on Earth* (Sydney: University of New South Wales Press, 2010)

Collins, Paul, *The Birth of the West: Rome, Germany, France, and the Creation of Europe in the Tenth Century* (New York: Public Affairs, 2013)

Cook, Francis H., "Heian, Kamakura, and Tokugawa Periods in Japan", Charles S. Prebish, ed., *Buddhism: A Modern Perspective* (University Park: Pennsylvania State University Press, 1975), 223-228

Cox, Harvey, "The Market as God: Living in the New Dispensation", *The Atlantic Monthly*, March 2009, digital edition

Daly, Herman E., Cobb, John B., *For the Common Good: Redirecting the Economy toward Community, the Environment and a Sustainable Future* (Boston: Beacon Press, 1989)

De Gruchy, John, *Christianity and Democracy: A Theology for a Just World Order* (Cambridge: Cambridge University Press, 1995)

Drew, Rose, *Buddhist and Christian? An Exploration of Dual Belonging* (London and New York: Routledge, 2011)

Duchrow, Ulrich, *Alternatives to Global Capitalism: Drawn from Biblical History, Designed for Political Action* (Utrecht: International Books; Heidelberg, Kairos Europa, 1995)

Bibliography

Dussel, Enrique, *Von der Erfindung Amerikas zur Entdeckung des Anderen* (Düsseldorf: Patmos, 1993 = Theologie Interkulturell 6)

Effendy, B., *Islam and the State in Indonesia* (Athens, Ohio: Ohio University Press; Singapore: Institute of Southeast Asian Studies, 2003)

Falk, Richard, "Humane Governance for the World: Reviving the Quest", Rorden Wilkinson, ed., *The Global Governance Reader* (London and New York: Routledge, 2005), 105-119

Falvey, Lindsay, *Religion and Agriculture: Sustainability in Christianity and Buddhism* (Adelaide: Institute for International Development, 2005)

Farhadian, C.E., *Christianity, Islam, and Nationalism in Indonesia* (New York and London: Routledge, 2005)

Federspiel, H.M., *Islam and Ideology in the Emerging Indonesian State: The Persetuan Islam (PERSIS), 1923 to 1957* (Leiden-Boston-Köln: Brill, 2001)

Fernando, L.A. Jude Lal, *Religion, Conflict and Peace in Sri Lanka: The Politics of Interpretation of Nationhoods* (Münster-Wien-Berlin: LIT Verlag, 2013)

Fletcher, Frank, *Jesus and the Dreaming: Discovering an Australian Spirituality Through Aboriginal-Christian Dialogue* (Strathfield: St Pauls Publications, 2013)

Fredericks, James, *Buddhists and Christians: Through Comparative Theology to Solidarity* (Maryknoll: Orbis Books, 2004)

Friedman, Thomas, "Democracy Worldwide Goes Deeper into Recession", *The Age* (Melbourne), 22/2/2015

Fugmann, Gernot, ed., *Ethics and Development in Papua New Guinea* (Goroka: The Melanesian Institute, 1986)

Gabriel, Klaus, "Das schnelle Geld. Die Spekulation als solche und ihre ethische Bewertung", Hoffmann, Johannes, and

Gerhard Scherhorn, eds, *Eine Politik für Nachhaltigkeit. Neuordnung der Kapital- und Gütermärkte* (Erkelenz: Altius Verlag, 2009), 220-236

Gammage, Bill, *The Biggest Estate on Earth: How Aborigines Made Australia* (Sydney: Allen & Unwin, 2012)

Gascoigne, Robert, "Christian Faith and the Public Forum in a Pluralist Society", *Colloquium* 26/2 (1994), 116-120

Gascoigne, Robert, *The Public Forum and Christian Ethics* (Cambridge: Cambridge University Press, 2001)

Gesch, Patrick V., *Initiative and Initiation: A Cargo Cult-Type Movement in the Sepik Against Its Background in Traditional Village Religion* (St. Augustin: Anthropos-Institut, 1985)

Giddings, Lynn, "Social Impact Study of the Yonki Hydro Scheme: Youth Rehabilitation Services Report", Fugmann, Gernot, ed., *Ethics and Development in Papua New Guinea* (Goroka: The Melanesian Institute, 1986), 149-201

Glancy, Brian, *Liberalism Without Secularism? Rachid Ghannouchi and the Theory and Politics of Islamic Democracy* (Dublin: Columba Press, 2007)

Goodhart, David, *The Road to Somewhere: The New Tribes Shaping British Politics* (Melbourne: Penguin Random House, 2017)

Goosen, Gideon, *Hyphenated Christians: Towards a Better Understanding of Dual Religious Belonging* (Bern: Peter Lang, 2011)

Habermas, Jürgen, *Strukturen der Öffentlichkeit* (Frankfurt: Suhrkamp, 1990, orig. 1962)

Hakamaya, Noriaki, "Scholarship as Criticism", Jamie Hubbard and Paul L. Swanson, eds, *Pruning the Bodhi Tree: The Storm over Critical Buddhism* (Honolulu: University of Hawaii Press, 1997), 113-144

Harris, Elizabeth J., "Confrontations over Conversions: A Case Study from Sri Lanka", John D'Arcy May, ed., *Converging Ways? Conversion and Belonging in Buddhism and Christianity* (St Ottilien: EOS Verlag, 2007), 37-54

Harris, Elizabeth J., *Theravāda Buddhism and the British Encounter: Religious, Missionary and Colonial Experience in Nineteenth Century Sri Lanka* (London and New York: Routledge, 2006)

Harris, Ian, ed., *Buddhism and Politics in Twentieth-Century Asia* (London and New York: Pinter, 1999)

Haynes, Jeff, *Religion in Third World Politics* (Buckingham and Philadelphia: Open University Press, 1993)

Hefner, Robert, *Civil Islam: Muslims and Democratization in Indonesia* (Princeton: Princeton University Press, 2000)

Held, David, "Democracy: From City-states to a Cosmopolitan Order?", *id.*, ed., *Prospects for Democracy: North, South, East, West* (Cambridge: Polity Press, 1993), 13-52

Herbert, David, *Religion and Civil Society: Rethinking Public Religion in the Contemporary World* (Aldershot: Ashgate, 2003)

Herschock, Peter D., *Buddhism in the Public Sphere: Reorienting Global Interdependence* (London and New York: Routledge, 2006)

Hettiarachchi, Shanthikumar, *Faithing the Native Soil: Dilemmas and Aspirations of Post-Colonial Buddhists and Christians in Sri Lanka* (Colombo: Centre for Society and Religion, 2012)

Hintersteiner, Norbert, "Intercultural and Interreligious (Un)Translatability and the Comparative Theology Project", *id.*, ed., *Naming and Thinking God in Europe Today: Theology in Global Dialogue* (Amsterdam and New York: Editions Rodopi, 2007), 465-491.

Hogan, Linda, und John D'Arcy May, "Gender and Culture as Dimensions of Bodiliness", Harm Goris, ed., *Bodiliness and Human Dignity: An Intercultural Approach / Leiblichkeit und Menschenwürde. Interkulturelle Zugänge* (Berlin: LIT Verlag, 2006), 45-57

Hogan, Linda, und John D'Arcy May, "Konstruktionen des Menschlichen. Würde im interreligiösen Dialog", Regina Ammicht-Quinn, Maureen Junker-Kenny und Elsa Tamez, eds, *Menschenwürde in der Debatte. Concilium* 39/2 (2003), 201-213

Hollenbach, David, *The Global Face of Public Faith: Politics, Human Rights, and Christian Ethics* (Washington, DC: Georgetown University Press, 2003)

Hooker, M.B., *Indonesian Islam: Social Change through Contemporary Fatawa* (Sydney: Allen & Unwin; Honolulu: University of Hawaii Press, 2003)

Houtart, François, and François Polet, *The Other Davos: Globalization of Resistances and Struggles* (Tiruvalla: Christava Sahitya Samithi, 2000)

Houtart, François, *Délégitimer le capitalisme. Reconstruire l'espérance* (Brüssel: Editions Colophon), 2005

Hoye, William J., *Demokratie und Christentum. Die christliche Verantwortung für demokratische Prinzipien* (Münster: Aschendorff, 1999)

Hudson, Wayne, *Australian Religious Thought* (Clayton: Monash University Publishing, 2016)

Humphreys, Stephen, *Climate Change and Human Rights: A Rough Guide* (Geneva: International Council on Human Rights Policy, 2008)

Ireeuw, T.M., "An Appeal for Melanesian Christian Solidarity", Garry W. Trompf, ed., *The Gospel is Not Western: Black Theologies from the Southwest Pacific* (Maryknoll: Orbis

Books, 1987), 170-182

Iserloh, Erwin, "Europe under the Sign of Confessional Pluralism", Erwin Iserloh, Josef Glazik, Hubert Jedin, eds, *Reformation and Counter Reformation, History of the Church, Vol. V* (London: Burns & Oates, 1980), 410-419

Jackson, Peter A., *Buddhism, Legitimation, and Conflict: The Political Functions of Urban Thai Buddhism* (Singapore: Institute of Southeast Asian Studies, 1989)

Jones, Ken, *The Social Face of Buddhism: An Approach to Political and Social Activism* (London: Wisdom Publications, 1989)

Kahn, Paul W., *Political Theology: Four New Chapters on the Concept of Sovereignty* (New York: Columbia University Press, 2011)

Kaldor, Mary, "The Idea of Global Civil Society", in: *International Affairs* 79/3 (2003), 583-593

Kaldor, Mary, *Global Civil Society: An Answer to War* (Cambridge: Polity Press, 2003)

Kant, Immanuel, *Zum ewigen Frieden. Ein philosophischer Entwurf* (Stuttgart: Reclam, 1973, orig. 1795)

Keane, John, *Global Civil Society?* (Cambridge: Cambridge University Press, 2003)

Keane, John, Review of Francis Fukuyama, *Political Order and Political Decay: From the Industrial Revolution to the Globalisation of Democracy*, in *The Age* (Melbourne), 14/2/2015

Keane, John, *The Life and Death of Democracy* (London-Sydney-New York-Toronto: Pocket Books [Simon and Schuster], 2009)

Knitter, Paul F., "Comparative Theology is not 'Business-as-Usual Theology': Personal Witness from a Buddhist Christian", *Buddhist-Christian Studies* 35 (2015), 181-192

Knitter, Paul F., *Without Buddha I Could Not Be a Christian* (Oxford und New York: OneWorld, 2009)

Küng, Hans, *Projekt Weltethos* (München-Zürich: Piper, 1990)

Küng, Hans, und Karl-Josef Kuschel, eds, *Erklärung zum Weltethos. Die Deklaration des Parlamentes der Weltreligionen* (München-Zürich: Piper, 1993)

Küng, Hans, und Karl-Josef Kuschel, eds, *Wissenschaft und Weltethos* (München-Zürich: Piper, 1998)

Leenhardt, Maurice, *Do Kamo. La personne et le mythe dans le monde mélanésien* (Paris: Gallimard, [1947] 1971)

Leith, Denise, *The Politics of Power: Freeport in Suharto's Indonesia* (Honolulu: University of Hawaii Press, 2003)

Loy, David R., review of Peter D. Herschock, *Buddhism in the Public Sphere: Reorienting Global Interdependence*, *Philosophy East and West* 58/1 (2008), 144-147

Loy, David, *A Buddhist History of the West: Studies in Lack* (Albany: State University of New York Press, 2002)

Madigan, Patricia, "Graced by Migration: An Australian Perspective", Elaine Padilla and Peter Phan, eds, *Christianities in Migration: The Global Perspective* (New York: Palgrave Macmillan, 2016), 135-152

Magliola, Robert, *Facing Up to Real Doctrinal Difference: How Some Motifs from Derrida can Nourish the Catholic-Buddhist Encounter* (Kettering, Ohio: Angelico Press, 2014)

Makransky, John, "Buddhist Inclusivism", Schmidt-Leukel, Perry, ed., *Buddhist Attitudes to Other Religions* (St Ottilien: EOS Verlag, 2008),

Manne, Robert, "How the fortress came to pass", *The Age* (Melbourne), 4/3/2018

Mantovani, Ennio, *The Dema and the Christ: My Engagement and Inner Dialogue with the Cultures and Religions of Melanesia* (Siegburg: Franz Schmitt Verlag, 2014)

Marshall, Andrew, *Thailand: A Kingdom in Crisis* (London: Zed Books, 2014)

Matsumoto, Shiro, "The Meaning of 'Zen'", Jamie Hubbard und Paul L. Swanson, eds, *Pruning the Bodhi Tree: The Storm over Critical Buddhism* (Honolulu: University of Hawaii Press, 1997), 242-250

Mawene, M.T., "Christ and Theology of Liberation in West Papua", *Exchange* 33 (2004), 153-179

May, John D'Arcy, "'Rights of the Earth' and 'Care for the Earth': Two Paradigms for a Buddhist-Christian Ecological Ethic", *Horizons* 21 (1994), 48-61

May, John D'Arcy, "'All in Each Place': Buddhist-Christian Relations at Home and Abroad", Schmidt-Leukel, Perry, ed., *Buddhist-Christian Relations in Asia* (Sankt Ottilien: EOS Verlag, 2017), 429-444

May, John D'Arcy, "Christian-Buddhist-Marxist Dialogue in Sri Lanka: A Model for Social Change in Asia?", *Journal of Ecumenical Studies* 19 (1982), 719-743

May, John D'Arcy, "Contested Space: Alternative Models of the Public Sphere in the Asia-Pacific", Neil Brown and Robert Gascoigne, eds, *Faith in the Public Forum* (Adelaide: Australian Theological Forum, 1999), 78-108

May, John D'Arcy, "Der Osten des Westens. Europa vor der Herausforderung des interreligiösen Dialogs", *Ost-West. Europäische Perspektiven* 3 (2002), 243-253

May, John D'Arcy, "Die ökumenische Alternative. Die eine bewohnte Erde neu denken", *Salzburger Theologische Zeitschrift* 14/2 (2010), 187-202

May, John D'Arcy, "Economics and Culture in the South Pacific: Some Presuppositions of Ethical Investment in Aboriginal and Melanesian Contexts", Project Group Ethical-Ecological Rating Frankfurt-Hohenheim, ed., *Intercultural*

Comparability of the Ethical Assessment of Enterprises According to Criteria of Cultural, Social and Environmental Responsibility (München: ökom Verlag, 2000), 70-76

May, John D'Arcy, "Economics and Culture in the South Pacific", Lucia A. Reisch, ed., *Ethical-ecological Investment: Towards Global Sustainable Development* (Frankfurt: IKO-Verlag für Interkulturelle Kommunikation, 2001), 117-122

May, John D'Arcy, "Ethic of Survival or Vision of Hope? The Aim of Interreligious Dialogue", *Dharma World* 29 (Sept.-Oct. 2002), 25-28

May, John D'Arcy, "Europe's God: Liberator or Oppressor? The Postcolonial Mediation of Transcendence", Norbert Hintersteiner, ed., *Naming and Thinking God in Europe Today: Theology in Global Dialogue* (Amsterdam and New York: Editions Rodopi, 2007), 69-92

May, John D'Arcy, "Gibt es eine buddhistische Wirtschaftsethik?", Maria Hungerkamp and Matthias Lutz, eds, *Grenzenüberschreitende Ethik. Festschrift für Prof. Dr. Johannes Hoffmann anlässlich seines 60. Geburtstages* (Frankfurt a.M.: IKO-Verlag für Interkulturelle Kommunikation, 1997), 65-82

May, John D'Arcy, "God in Public: The Religions in Pluralist Societies", *Bijdragen: International Journal in Philosophy and Theology* 64/3 (2003), 249-264

May, John D'Arcy, "Human Dignity, Human Rights, and Religious Pluralism: Buddhist and Christian Perspectives", *Buddhist-Christian Studies* 26 (2006), 51-60

May, John D'Arcy, "Initiation, Initiationsverlust und Initiationsersatz im Südpazifik", Thomas Schreijäck, ed., *Menschwerden im Kulturwandel. Kontexte kultureller Identität als Wegmarken interkultureller Kompetenz* (Luzern: Edition Exodus, 1999), 456-471

May, John D'Arcy, "Jakarta and Jayapura: The Dialogue of Religions and 'Papua, Land of Peace'", Carole M. Cusack and Christopher Hartney, eds, *Religion and Retributive Logic: Essays in Honour of Professor Garry W. Trompf* (Leiden and Boston: Brill, 2010), 19-42

May, John D'Arcy, "Mehr als Schulung. Religiöses Lernen als Identitätsstiftung im Südpazifik", Engelbert Groß and Klaus König, eds, *Religiöses Lernen der Kirchen im globalen Dialog. Weltweit akute Herausforderungen und Praxis einer Weggemeinschaft für Eine-Welt-Religionspädagogik* (Münster-Hamburg-London: LIT Verlag, 2000), 107-121

May, John D'Arcy, "Menschenrechte als Landrechte im Pazifik. Vier Fallstudien", Johannes Hoffmann, ed., *Universale Menschenrechte im Widerspruch der Kulturen. Das eine Menschenrecht für alle und die vielen Lebensformen*, Vol. II (Frankfurt: IKO-Verlag für interkulturelle Kommunikation, 1994), 213-237

May, John D'Arcy, "Pacifism: Historical Phenomenon and Philosophical Problem", Norman Habel, ed., *Remembering Pioneer Australian Pacifist Charles Strong* (Northcote, Vic.: Morning Star, 2018), 41-54.

May, John D'Arcy, "Political Religion: Secularity and the Study of Religion in Global Civil Society", Basia Spalek and Alia Imtoual, eds, *Religion, Spirituality and the Social Sciences: Challenging Marginalisation* (Bristol: Policy Press, 2008), 9-22

May, John D'Arcy, "Political Theology Revisited", O'Grady, John; Cathy Higgins; Jude Lal Fernando, eds, *Mining Truths: Festschrift in Honour of Geraldine Smyth OP – Ecumenical Theologian and Peacebuilder* (St. Ottilien: EOS Verlag, 2015), 537-554

May, John D'Arcy, "Rootedness: Reflections on Land and Belonging", Werner Jeanrond und Andrew D.H. Mays, eds, *Recognising the Margins: Developments in Biblical and Theological Studies. Essays in Honour of Seán Freyne* (Dublin: Columba Press, 2006), 146-159

May, John D'Arcy, "The Globalisation of Theology", Price, Peter, ed., *A World United or a World Exploited? Christian Perspectives on Globalisation* (Adelaide: Australian Theological Forum, 2013 = *Interface* 16/2), 64-80

May, John D'Arcy, "The Religions and the Powers in West Papua", Amélé Adamavi-Aho Ekué und Michael Biehl, eds, *Gottesgabe. Vom Geben und Nehmen im Kontext gelebter Religion. Festschrift zum 65. Geburtstag von Theodor Ahrens* (Frankfurt: Lembeck, 2005), 199-213

May, John D'Arcy, "Towards the Development of Ethics", *Catalyst* 17 (1987), 235-251

May, John D'Arcy, "Vorbereitende Überlegungen zu einer Konsenstheorie der Konziliarität", *Una Sancta* 32 (1977), 94-104

May, John D'Arcy, "Whatever Happened to the Melanesian Council of Churches? A Study in Ecumenical Organisation", *Melanesian Journal of Theology* 1 (1985), 138-157

May, John D'Arcy, "Whose Universality? Which Interdependence? Human Rights, Social Responsibility and Ecological Integrity", Jacques Haers SJ, Norbert Hintersteiner and Georges De Schrijver SJ, eds, *Postcolonial Europe in the Crucible of Cultures: Reckoning with God in a World of Conflicts* (Amsterdam and New York: Rodopi, 2007), 193-211

May, John D'Arcy, *After Pluralism: Towards an Interreligious Ethic* (Münster-Hamburg-London: LIT Verlag, 2000)

May, John D'Arcy, and Linda Hogan, "Constructing the Human: Dignity in Interreligious Dialogue", Regina Ammicht-Quinn, Maureen Junker-Kenny and Elsa Tamez, eds, *The Discourse of Human Dignity* (London: SCM, Concilium 2003/2), 78-89

May, John D'Arcy, and Linda Hogan, "Visioning Ecumenics as Intercultural, Inter-religious, and Public Theology", Linda Hogan, Solange Lefebvre, Norbert Hintersteiner, Felix Wilfred, eds, *Concilium: From World Mission to Inter-religious Witness* (London: SCM, 2011), 70-81

May, John D'Arcy, *Buddhologie und Christologie. Unterwegs zu einer kollaborativen Theologie* (Innsbruck-Wien: Tyrolia Verlag, 2014)

May, John D'Arcy, *Christus Initiator. Theologie im Pazifik* (Düsseldorf: Patmos, 1990 = Theologie Interkulturell 4)

May, John D'Arcy, ed., *Converging Ways? Conversion and Belonging in Buddhism and Christianity* (St Ottilien: EOS Verlag, 2007)

May, John D'Arcy, *Imagining the Ecumenical: A Personal Journey* (Northcote, Vic.: Morning Star, 2016)

May, John D'Arcy, review of Magliola, Robert, *Facing Up to Real Doctrinal Difference*, Buddhist-Christian Studies 35 (2015), 238-241

May, John D'Arcy, *Transcendence and Violence: The Encounter of Buddhist, Christian and Primal Traditions* (London and New York: Continuum, 2003)

McCormack, Gavan, *The Emptiness of Japanese Affluence* (St Leonards: Allen & Unwin, 1996)

McCulloch, J.A., *Comparative Theology* (London: Methuen, 1902)

McGarry, Patsy, *The Irish Times* (Dublin), 23/12/2014 [on the persecution of Christians]

McMullin, Neil, "The *Lotus Sutra* and Politics in the Mid-Heian Period", George J. Tanabe Jr. und Willa Jane Tanabe, ed., *The Lotus Sutra in Japanese Culture* (Honolulu: University of Hawaii Press, 1989), 119-141

Metz, Johann Baptist, "Compassion. Zu einem Weltprogramm des Christentums im Zeitalter des Pluralismus der Religionen und Kulturen", *id. et al.*, eds, *Compassion. Weltprogramm des Christentums. Soziale Verantwortung lernen* (Freiburg-Basel-Wien: Herder, 2000), 9-18

Miller, Nick, "Dawn of the Demagogues: Is Democracy Winning or Losing the Global Contest?", *The Sunday Age* (Melbourne), 25/2/2018

Murdoch, Lindsay, "'Hundreds' of Rohingya villages destroyed", *The Age* (Melbourne), 19/12/2017; "Devastation must be seen to be understood", *The Age*, 27/12/2017

Nagel, Tilman, *Staat und Glaubensgemeinschaft im Islam. Geschichte der politischen Ordnungsvorstellungen der Muslime. Band I: Von den Anfängen bis ins 13. Jahrhundert* (Zürich-München: Artemis, 1981)

Nash, Roderick F., *The Rights of Nature: A History of Environmental Ethics* (Madison: University of Wisconsin Press, 1989)

Nuttal, G.F., *Christian Pacifism in History* (Oxford: Blackwell, 1958)

Owen, N.G., ed., *The Emergence of Modern Southeast Asia: A New History* (Honolulu: University of Hawaii Press, 2005)

Pascoe, Bruce, *Dark Emu: Aboriginal Australia and the Birth of Agriculture* (Broome: Magabala Books, rev. ed. 2018)

Pawlikowski, John, "Vatican II's Theological About-face on the Jews: Not yet fully recognized", *The Ecumenist* 37 (2000), 4-6

Petito, Fabio, and Pavlos Hatzopoulos, eds, *Religion in International Relations: The Return from Exile* (New York: Palgrave Macmillan, 2003)

Phongphit, Seri, *Religion in a Changing Society: Buddhism, Reform and the Role of Monks in Community Development* (Hong Kong: Arena Press, 1988)

Pye, Michael, *The Buddha* (London: Duckworth, 1979)

Queen, Christopher S., and Sallie B. King, eds, *Engaged Buddhism: Buddhist Liberation Movements in Asia* (Albany: State University of New York Press, 1996)

Reynolds, Noel B., und W. Cole Durham Jr., eds, *Religious Liberty in Western Thought* (Atlanta: Scholars Press, 1996)

Ridgeon, Lloyd and Perry Schmidt-Leukel, eds, *Islam and Inter-Faith Relations* (London: SCM, 2007)

Robbins, Jeffrey W., *Radical Democracy and Political Theology* (New York: Columbia University Press, 2011)

Said, Edward, *Culture and Imperialism* (London: Vintage, 1994)

Said, Edward, *Orientalism: Western Conceptions of the Orient* (London: Penguin, 1991, orig. 1978)

Saleh, F., *Modern Trends in Islamic Theological Discourse in Twentieth Century Indonesia: A Critical Survey* (Leiden: Brill, 2001)

Saltford, John, *The United Nations and the Indonesian Takeover of West Papua, 1962-1969: The Anatomy of Betrayal* (London and New York: Routledge Curzon, 2003)

Scherhorn, Gerhard, *Nachhaltige Entwicklung. Die besondere Verantwortung des Finanzkapitals / Sustainable development: The outstanding responsibility of financial capital* (Erkelenz: Altius Verlag, 2008)

Scherhorn, Gerhard, *Wachstum oder Nachhaltigkeit. Die Ökonomie am Scheideweg* (Erkelenz: Altius Verlag, 2015)

Schmidt-Leukel, Perry, "Limits and Prospects of Comparative Theology", Norbert Hintersteiner, ed., *Naming and Thinking God in Europe Today: Theology in Global Dialogue* (Amsterdam and New York: Editions Rodopi, 2007), 493-505

Schmidt-Leukel, Perry, ed., *Buddhist-Christian Relations in Asia* (Sankt Ottilien: EOS Verlag, 2017)

Schmitt, Carl, *Political Theology: Four Chapters on the Concept of Sovereignty* (Chicago and London: University of Chicago Press, 1985), translated by George Schwab from the revised German edition of 1934.

Scholte, Jan Aart, "Civil Society and Democracy in Global Governance", Rorden Wilkinson, ed., *The Global Governance Reader* (London/New York: Routledge, 2005), 322-340

Schulmeister, Stephan, "Destabilisierende Finanzspekulation und ihre Eindämmung durch eine Transaktionssteuer", Hoffmann, Johannes, and Gerhard Scherhorn, eds, *Eine Politik für Nachhaltigkeit. Neuordnung der Kapital- und Gütermärkte* (Erkelenz: Altius Verlag, 2009), 197-219

Schwarz, Nick, *Thinking Critically about Sorcery and Witchcraft: A Handbook for Christians in Papua New Guinea* (Goroka: The Melanesian Institute, 2011, rev. 2013)

Schweiker, William, *Theological Ethics and Global Dynamics: In the Time of Many Worlds* (Oxford: Blackwell, 2004)

Sedlacek, Thomas, *Economics of Good and Evil: The Quest for Economic Meaning from Gilgamesh to Wall Street* (New York: Oxford University Press, 2011)

Sen, Amartya, *On Ethics and Economics* (Oxford: Blackwell, 1988)

Sharpe, Eric, *Comparative Religion: A History* (London: Duckworth, 1975)

Sinn, Simone, *Religiöser Pluralismus im Werden. Religionspolitische Kontroversen und theologische Perspektiven von Christen und Muslimen in Indonesien* (Tübingen: Mohr Siebeck, 2014)

Sivaraksa, Sulak, ed., *Radical Conservatism: Buddhism in the Contemporary World. Articles in Honour of Bhikkhu Buddhadasa's 84th Birthday Anniversary* (Bangkok: Thai Inter-Religious Commission for Development, International Network of Engaged Buddhists, 1990)

Sivaraksa, Sulak, *Siamese Resurgence: A Thai Buddhist Voice on Asia and a World of Change* (Bangkok: Asian Cultural Forum on Development, 1985)

Sivaraksa, Sulak, *The Wisdom of Sustainability: Buddhist Economics for the 21st Century* (Kihei, Hawaii: Koa Books, 2009)

Sizemore, Russell F., and Donald K. Swearer, eds, *Ethics, Wealth and Salvation: A Study in Buddhist Social Ethics* (Columbia, SC: University of South Carolina Press, 1990)

Smith, Wilfred Cantwell, *Towards a World Theology: Faith and the Comparative History of Religion* (London: Macmillan, 1981)

Stiglitz, Joseph, *Globalization and Its Discontents* (New York: Norton, 2002)

Stiglitz, Joseph, *The Price of Inequality* (London: Allen Lane, 2012)

Stobbe, Heinz-Günther, "Einheit der Kirche, ökumenische Forschung und Systemtheorie", Thomas Bremer und Maria Wernsmann, eds, *Ökumene – Überdacht. Reflexionen und Realitäten im Umbruch* (Freiburg-Basel-Wien: Herder, 2014 = Quaestiones Disputatae 259), 37-73

Stobbe, Heinz-Günther, *Religion, Gewalt und Krieg. Eine Einführung* (Stuttgart: Kohlhammer, 2010)

Stockton, Eugene, "Eine erd-gesinnte Spiritualität im heutigen Australien", Hans Kessler, ed., *Ökologisches Weltethos im Dialog der Kulturen und Religionen* (Darmstadt: Wissenschaftliche Buchgesellschaft, 1996), 183-195

Stockton, Eugene, *The Aboriginal Gift: Spirituality for a Nation* (Alexandria, NSW: Millennium Books, 1995)

Stockton, Eugene, *The Deep Within: Towards an Archetypal Theology* (Lawson: Blue Mountains Education and Research Trust, 2011)

Stosch, Klaus von, "Comparative Theology as an Alternative to the Theology of Religions", Norbert Hintersteiner, ed., *Naming and Thinking God in Europe Today: Theology in Global Dialogue* (Amsterdam and New York: Editions Rodopi, 2007), 507-512

Stout, Jeffrey, *Democracy and Tradition* (Princeton and Oxford: Princeton University Press, 2004)

Stowe, Judith A., *Siam Becomes Thailand: A Story of Intrigue* (Honolulu: University of Hawaii Press, 1991)

Strelan, John, *Search for Salvation: Studies in the History and Theology of Cargo Cults* (Adelaide: Lutheran Publishing House, 1977)

Sullivan, William M., and Will Kymlicka, eds, *The Globalization of Ethics* (Cambridge: Cambridge University Press, 2007)

Swain, Tony, "Reinventing the Eternal: Aboriginal Spirituality and Modernity", Normal C. Habel, ed., *Religion and Multiculturalism in Australia: Essays in Honour of Victor Hayes* (Adelaide: Australian Association for the Study of Religions, 1992), 122-136

Swain, Tony, *A Place for Strangers: Towards a History of Aboriginal Being* (Cambridge: Cambridge University Press, 1993)

Swidler, Leonard, *After the Absolute: The Dialogical Future of Religion* (Minneapolis: Fortress Press, 1990)

Swidler, Leonard, ed., *Toward a Universal Theology of Religion* (Maryknoll: Orbis Books, 1987)

Swift, Louis J., ed., *The Early Fathers on War and Military Service* (Wilmington, Delaware: Glazier, 1983)

Tacey, David, *Beyond Literal Belief: Religion as Metaphor* (Melbourne: John Garratt Publishing, 2015)

Tacey, David, *Edge of the Sacred: Transformation in Australia* (Melbourne: HarperCollins, 1995)

Tambiah, S. J., *Buddhism and the Spirit Cults in North-east Thailand* (Cambridge: Cambridge University Press, 1970)

Tambiah, S.J., *World Conqueror and World Renouncer: A Study of Buddhism and Polity in Thailand against a Historical Background* (Cambridge: Cambridge University Press, 1976)

Taylor, Charles, *A Secular Age* (Cambridge, Mass. and London: The Belknap Press of Harvard University Press, 2007)

Tebay, Neles, *Interfaith Endeavours for Peace in West Papua* (Aachen: Missio, 2006)

Tehranian, Majid, "A Muslim View of Buddhism", Ridgeon, Lloyd and Perry Schmidt-Leukel, eds, *Islam and Inter-Faith Relations* (London: SCM, 2007), 213-224

Tierney, Brian, *Foundations of the Conciliar Theory: The Contribution of the Medieval Canonists from Gratian to the Great Schism* (Cambridge: Cambridge University Press, 1955)

Tocqueville, Alexis de, *De la Démocratie en Amérique* (Paris: Union Générale, 1963)

Triffitt, Mark, "Beware of Democracy's Retreat behind Walls", *The Age* (Melbourne), 14/3/2016

Trompf, Garry W., *Melanesian Religion* (Cambridge: Cambridge University Press, 1991)

Trompf, Garry, *Payback: The Logic of Retribution in Melanesian Religions* (Cambridge: Cambridge University Press, 1994)

Ungunmerr, Miriam Rose, "*Dadirri*", Stockton, Eugene, *The Aboriginal Gift: Spirituality for a Nation* (Alexandria, NSW: Millennium Books, 1995), Appendix 1, 179-184

Vallely, Paul, *The Independent* (London), 27/7/2014 [on the persecution of Christians]

Victoria, Brian, *Zen at War* (New York/Tokyo: Weatherhill, 1997)

Ward, Tony, *Bridging Troubled Waters: Australia and Asylum Seekers* (North Melbourne: Australian Scholarly Publishing, 2017)

Williamson, Raymond K., *Pilgrims of Hope: An Ecumenical Journey 1980-2010* (Northcote, Vic.: Morning Star, 2014)

Wilson, Martin, *New, Old and Timeless: Pointers Toward an Aboriginal Theology* (Kensington: Chevalier Press, 1979)

Winkler, Ulrich, "Für eine pneumatologische Religionstheologie", *Salzburger Theologische Zeitschrift* 11/2 (2007), 175-200

Winkler, Ulrich, "Komparative Theologie der Religionen", *Salzburger Theologische Zeitschrift* 11/2 (2007), 137-139

www.ingramcontent.com/pod-product-compliance
Lightning Source LLC
Chambersburg PA
CBHW051942290426
44110CB00015B/2082